Imperfect Heroes

Imperfect Heroes

Teaching in Challenging Times to Motivate Student Achievement

Andrew Barkley

ROWMAN & LITTLEFIELD
Lanham • Boulder • New York • London

Published by Rowman & Littlefield
An imprint of The Rowman & Littlefield Publishing Group, Inc.
4501 Forbes Boulevard, Suite 200, Lanham, Maryland 20706
www.rowman.com

86-90 Paul Street, London EC2A 4NE, United Kingdom

British Library Cataloguing in Publication Information Available

Library of Congress Cataloging-in-Publication Data

Names: Barkley, Andrew P., 1962– author.
Title: Imperfect heroes : teaching in challenging times to motivate student achievement /
    Andrew Barkley.
Description: Lanham, Maryland : Rowman & Littlefield, 2022. | Summary: "This book
    is a reflective meditation on everyday teaching, sharing the joys and pain of an
    educator's journey"—Provided by publisher.
Identifiers: LCCN 2021048563 (print) | LCCN 2021048564 (ebook) |
    ISBN 9781475862065 (cloth) | ISBN 9781475862072 (paperback) |
    ISBN 9781475862089 (epub)
Subjects: LCSH: Teaching—Psychological aspects. | Academic achievement. |
    Motivation in education. | Role models.
Classification: LCC LB1027 .B255 8 2022 (print) | LCC LB1027 (ebook) |
    DDC 370.15—dc23/eng/20211109
LC record available at https://lccn.loc.gov/2021048563
LC ebook record available at https://lccn.loc.gov/2021048564

Dedication
To Margaret Cates Freeman (1964–2016) and Ray Freeman.
Dedicated, caring, and inspiring educators. Teaching heroes.

Contents

Foreword

More than a decade ago at a mid-winter faculty development retreat organized by my university, I heard Andy Barkley talk with a group of dedicated teachers about Willie Nelson. Yes, that Willie Nelson, the long-haired music star famous for many things, including the outlaw country sound that fused classic country, honky-tonk, the blues, and rock. As an unapologetic fan, I was intrigued but also slightly perplexed about the relevance of Willie to post-secondary teaching.

Barkley told the story of how Nelson, a successful Nashville songwriter but also a suit-and-tie-wearing country music performer with a string of minor hits in the 1960s, suffered stage fright and felt suffocated by the formulaic sounds and styles of Nashville in its countrypolitan period. He had to leave, "retiring" before he was yet forty and moving to Austin, where he realized that he had to dress and look the way he felt comfortable (inspired by Austin's hippie scene) and to make the kind of music that made him (rather than Nashville executives) excited and happy. In the decade that followed, Nelson released *Shotgun Willie*, *Red Headed Stranger*, *Stardust*, and so much more, and went from being a successful songwriter and forgettable performer to an American music legend, whose love of touring, live performances, and fans is renowned.

Barkley's point wasn't that Willie Nelson is awesome. His emphasis instead was on Nelson's imperfections and his struggles. Despite his talent, he struggled as a performer in the 1960s, and he didn't become great until he figured out how to be at ease with himself and to accept himself as he was, until he started to sing what *he* wanted to say. And this self-acceptance—this authenticity, if you will—is precisely what enabled Nelson to feel comfortable enough and brave enough to connect with his audiences in his personal, genuine, take-each-other-as-we-are manner.

I learned a lot during that talk, and it wasn't only new insights on Nelson's shift from countrypolitan to outlaw country. It turned out that Barkley's point was all about teaching after all. He was urging us not just to be ourselves in the classroom but to use a kind of personal authenticity or self-acceptance as a way to unleash the energy and creativity that would help us become not just successful teachers but exceptional ones. He was teaching us how to overcome fear of others by connecting with others. In telling the story of how Nelson taught himself to make eye contact with at least one fan in the audience, and then another and another, and then to point and wave and smile at those fans, Barkley was teaching us that we can start to vanquish our own stage fright in the classroom with tiny steps: making eye contact, greeting students by name, asking them how they're doing and listening. In the process, Barkley had used Nelson's personal narrative to take us from macro wisdom about identity and authenticity to micro teaching practices that can be effectively used in lots of classrooms. Since then and to this day, I remind myself, especially when I start to feel butterflies before class, to make eye contact with one student, to reach out and connect, then with another and another.

I recall my memory of this talk because it epitomizes Barkley's personal, highly originally, and genuinely remarkable method for teaching other teachers, in person, in lectures, and in this book that you're now reading. He begins with a biographical account of a great cultural figure and then culls from that life story a set of lessons about teaching, exploring along the way the relationships between these iconic heroes and teaching as a practice, a challenging and always imperfect but sometimes joyful practice. Barkley's emphasis is typically on the imperfections and obstacles, the hurdles or difficulties that lead us into new territory where we surprise ourselves by learning new things about teaching and ourselves.

This genre, serial biography, used to discover larger truths and new insights, has its roots in antiquity (Plutarch's *Lives*, Diogenes Laertius's *Lives of Eminent Philosophers*) as well as its medieval examples (lives of the saints) and modern masterpieces (Lytton Strachey's *Eminent Victorians*). Barkley's invention within the form is to use such biographical sketches to articulate in memorable ways the teaching practices that enhance student learning. I find this innovation original and powerful. For instance, the book is written by a passionate, sincere, and experienced teacher for other teachers, of all kinds. Teachers are typically lovers of learning. They enjoy exploring and discovering and letting their curiosity loose. They enjoy the experience of knowing new things and then reflecting on that knowledge for what practical wisdom it might hold. Each of Barkley's chapters offers us the opportunity to learn more about eminent figures like Nelson Mandela or Frida Kahlo or

Fred Rogers. While satisfying our epistemophilia, the chapters also allow us to learn new pedagogical practices, reflect on well-known ones in order to adapt or adopt them, and to think critically about our teaching or our relationship with our students or profession. In other words, knowing his audience or students well, Barkley has adopted a genre suited to them, a teaching style that will work with this class.

Barkley's imperfect heroes are selected from a pantheon of cultural figures that would be well known to many twenty-first-century readers and teachers. He presents them as his heroes, but they are truly iconic figures, whom we are likely to know about, even if we are not experts on any. Again, Barkley knows his students well. He activates our prior knowledge (as a Willie Nelson fan, I knew plenty) and builds on it (but I didn't at the time know about the unhappy start to his career as a Nashville performer); and then he uses this new knowledge to lead us to something quite unexpected, that thing we didn't know (how to cope and perhaps even overcome teaching anxiety, for example). On the one hand, this is a classic teaching technique, deployed by many great teachers. On the other hand, it's worth pointing out that *Imperfect Heroes'* genre is a deliberate pedagogical technique used to make this teaching guidance memorable. Throughout this book, you'll find, Barkley practices what he preaches.

Readers will also notice how Barkley systematically uses epigrams or inspiring quotations in each chapter. It might seem as if Barkley is adapting another ancient but enduring genre, the commonplace book, in which compilers collect quotations and proverbs among other fragments, including sometimes the compilers' own reflections. *Imperfect Heroes* could be seen as Barkley's own twenty-first-century commonplace book with quotations and reflections about teaching, arranged by themes and lives. Yet what I see again is a teacher who knows his students well, a teacher who knows that all learning ultimately depends on the students themselves who must always do the learning themselves. Hence the aim of the teacher is to motivate and inspire students to do their own learning. The quotations along with the life stories collected here are meant ultimately to inspire us, to make us curious enough and brave enough to learn new things and try new things. These chapters in their very design exemplify great teaching. They model for us how to teach well. But even more importantly, they encourage us to become curious, to care about our students, and to learn something new. In the process, they inspire us to improve our teaching in ways that feel authentic and foster connection to students.

—Gregory Eiselein
Professor and University Distinguished Teaching Scholar
Kansas State University

Preface

I wrote *Imperfect Heroes* with the hope of helping teachers flourish during challenging times. The book is written for all educators, but especially those who seek renewal in their ability to help students learn and grow. Throughout my teaching career, I have been inspired, motivated, and encouraged by the lives of my personal heroes featured here. Successful leaders, writers, and artists face challenges strikingly similar to obstacles faced by teachers. Iconic individuals often use life hardships as a springboard to achieve higher levels of effectiveness. Teachers can do this, too.

Personal, career, and relational roadblocks are universal, and much can be learned from how heroes have turned trials into successes. The main idea of this book is that learning about the lives of people different from ourselves can provide large benefits. The application of ideas from new and divergent sources to our teaching practices can result in transformative growth in our ability to help others learn. My hope is that teachers will use the hero stories intertwined with classroom examples to gain confidence, motivate students, and renew their commitment to making a positive contribution to the world.

In each chapter, I share common teaching experiences to stimulate reflection, dialog, and action. Emphasized throughout the book is my conviction that any teacher who desires to improve can become a great teacher, regardless of personality type, classroom style, subject matter, or pedagogical tools. My strong belief is that advocacy of student achievement through intention and inspiration can be a teacher's largest contribution to the world. This is the underlying theme and take-home message of *Imperfect Heroes*.

This is not a book on specific teaching methods, or practical advice on "how to teach." Instead, my message is a reflective meditation on everyday teaching, sharing the joys and pain of an educator's journey. The book is at once a biography of teaching heroes, a professional development book for teachers, and an inspirational volume. I have grounded the book in current, timely scholarship of teaching and educational research. The continuing importance of social justice is emphasized throughout the book.

Teaching experiences during isolation, confinement, and crisis are explored, and ideas about teaching during a crisis are shared, including consistency, transparency, and extravagant mercy. An ongoing characteristic of my teaching is making mistakes. As a result, the book surveys human deficiencies from many perspectives and philosophical traditions to provide strategies for advancement during difficult situations and challenging times. The book analyzes how faults, limitations, mistakes, and weaknesses can be sources for personal growth.

Students and teachers often reach their fullest potential by turning hardship into success. My sincere hope is that the book's message of overcoming obstacles will contribute to teachers as they help others to learn and grow. Teaching is difficult. Educators persist, knowing that a better future depends on the knowledge and experience of their students. Teachers benefit from reviewing shared classroom successes and failures. Readers of this book will explore common challenges, doubt, and victories, providing motivation to use today's teaching experience to teach again tomorrow, better than today.

This book is written for dedicated teachers across the world who eagerly desire to become more effective at helping students learn and grow. This is a large group, as evidenced by the hard work, dedication, and professionalism of teachers everywhere. My hope is that readers will take away from the twelve teaching heroes a strong desire to improve their teaching to promote student achievement. I have done my best to share some simple ideas about how to get started on the road to becoming a teaching hero. Keep going . . . you can do this!

Introduction

The book is organized in a simple fashion intended to maximize inspiration for readers. Each chapter describes how one teaching hero motivates improvement in teaching and learning. Each chapter begins with a "Synopsis" of what will be covered, and concludes with a "Teaching Summary" of hero characteristics that could be adopted to enhance educators' ability to improve student learning outcomes. An "Intersections" piece is also included at the end of each chapter that shows unexpected and meaningful connections across the twelve heroes.

Chapter 1 focuses on classroom presentations, using the life of boxing champion Muhammad Ali. The story of Ali provides motivation and inspiration for teachers to turn challenges into successes. Ali's battle for personal greatness and social justice provides an inspiring example for teachers to fight oppression and seek to have a positive impact on students and the world. Musician Bob Dylan's constant makeovers and genre changes provide the foundation for chapter 2. Teachers are encouraged to continuously adopt new methods, take on new challenges, and remain enthusiastic about student learning throughout their careers.

Turning failures into success is the topic of chapter 3. Mister Rogers provides an excellent role model for dealing with mistakes, sharing the idea that one cannot teach without making mistakes. This is powerful knowledge. Failure in performance faced by rock star Patti Smith is described and analyzed to enhance teachers' ability to overcome mistakes. Chapter 4 describes how Mother Teresa suffered deep personal doubts about her own religion and spirituality, yet continued her inspiring charity work throughout her life. Knowledge of Teresa's lifetime struggle can help teachers move forward in times of difficulty.

Chapter 5 shares Malcolm X's powerful story of how injustice and oppression create anger, and how Malcolm X transformed his immense anger into forgiveness. The National Memorial for Peace and Justice is described to examine the causes and consequences of systemic racism, and what teachers could do to move our world toward greater justice. In chapter 6, powerful lessons for teaching are gleaned from consideration of philosopher and writer Albert Camus' search for light in dark times. Camus' solution to the absurdity of life was humanity, decency, and good sense.

Chapter 7 highlights our sense of place, and student-teacher relationships using Chief Joseph's dignity, grace, and kindness. Nez Perce history is used to exemplify strategies for classroom management and relationships. Chapter 8 highlights how Nelson Mandela forgave his oppressors, and worked together with his enemies to forge the new "Rainbow Nation" of South Africa. The educational concept of challenge and support is presented with examples drawn from Mandela's life and work.

Mahatma Gandhi fought to end injustice and oppression in South Africa and India. Chapter 9 explores Gandhi's emphasis on win-win solutions. Anne Frank's powerful diary entries, summarized in chapter 10, illuminate how to successfully navigate life during unusual circumstances. Anne's pervasive optimism is highlighted, with special attention to remote teaching and online learning.

Chapter 11 shares important lessons from Martin Luther King, Jr. for teachers about racial relationships, and using this knowledge to make the world a better place. The final chapter describes Mexican artist Frida Kahlo, who faced enormous physical, emotional, and relational challenges throughout her life and career. Her inspiring life story provides motivation for teachers to minimize the effects of life struggles and enthusiastically promote student achievement through joy. Kahlo's cheerful support for her students is a powerful model for teachers to share positivity, encouragement, and enthusiasm with all students.

Chapter 1

Courage from Fear

Muhammad Ali

Figure 1.1   Muhammad Ali Wikimedia Commons. *Source*: *World Journal Tribune* photo by Ira Rosenberg. United States Library of Congress's Prints and Photographs division, digital ID cph.3c15435. *New York World-Telegram and the Sun* Newspaper Photograph Collection. http://hdl.loc.gov/loc.pnp/cph.3c15435

Float like a butterfly, sting like a bee.

—Muhammad Ali refrain.[1]

A fierce fighter and a man of peace.

—George W. Bush, honoring Muhammad
Ali with the Presidential Medal of Freedom,
the nation's highest civilian honor.[2]

CHAPTER SYNOPSIS

The life of boxer Muhammad Ali provides motivation and inspiration for teachers to transform challenges into successes. Ali's battle for social justice and personal greatness provides an inspiring example for teachers to fight injustice and seek to have a positive impact on their students and on the world. This chapter focuses on lectures, classroom presentations, and speeches. To illustrate how courage can conquer fear, Ali's boxing career and his lesser-known career as a public speaker at colleges and universities are explored.

Teaching provokes anxiety. Teachers of all ages, subjects, and experience levels can feel a crippling mix of fear, worry, and nervous energy as the beginning of class approaches. Once the class or lecture gets started, the fear often fades as teachers begin to practice their craft: sharing knowledge with students. As class proceeds, fear is replaced with euphoria: classroom interaction results in the deep satisfaction of sharing useful knowledge with others. Anxiety has some advantages. Teachers can use nervous energy to prepare carefully and extensively, resulting in better classes and more student learning.

The transformation of anxiety into successful performance occurs not only in classroom teaching but also in unexpected places such as professional sports. Muhammad Ali, the world heavyweight boxing champion, held the world's rapt attention throughout his life. Boxing fans and boxing opponents alike were ensnared by Ali's larger-than-life personality, outrageous proclamations, and unparalleled physical beauty, grace, and presence. Ali was talented, intelligent, and articulate. How did people know this? Because Muhammad Ali told them so. Loudly. Repeatedly. Boldly.

The world was at once captivated and repulsed by Ali's audacious, persistent rants, rhymes, and showmanship. Many found Ali's irreverence provocative and inspiring. How could anyone ignore an individual who claimed, "I am the greatest," and so clearly believed that he was, providing verbal evidence at every opportunity? Ali was bursting with energy, power, and independence. Ali was in equal parts entertaining and inspirational at the highest level: truly, the "Greatest of All Time."

Ali's intelligence, athleticism, and confidence allowed him to become a successful boxer. His engaging personality permitted him to leverage his boxing success to become famous well beyond his victories in the ring. And, later, Ali was able to transform his success and fame into the advancement of social causes.

Many ardent admirers of Ali are not boxing fans. Boxing is dangerous, and a large body of research provides evidence that repeated blows to the body and head can cause enormous physical, intellectual, and emotional damage. However, many pacifists remain huge fans of Muhammad Ali. Ali was contradictory, even about his own profession: "You know I hate fighting. If I knew how to make a living some other way, I would."[3] This duality mirrors the complex relationship between fear and courage in a lecture or classroom presentation.

Paradox is a recurring theme of teaching practice and experience. Teaching is a mystifying and inexplicable fusion of polarities: fear and courage; rational thought and emotion; private ideas and public performances; success and failure. Perhaps, to comprehend, assimilate, and manage the craft of teaching requires a larger-than-life, complex, contradictory, challenging hero. Maybe teaching requires floating like a butterfly and stinging like a bee.

Muhammad Ali became much more than a boxer when in 1964, after becoming the world heavyweight champion, he changed his religion by joining the Nation of Islam, and changed his name from his given name of Cassius Clay to Muhammad Ali. Ali continued to provoke and fascinate until he was the most widely recognized sports personality the world has ever known.

Fear was a constant theme throughout Ali's life. The unfair treatment of African Americans in the United States caused fear in the young Cassius Clay: "I used to lay awake scared, thinking about somebody getting cut up or being lynched. Look like they was always black people I liked. And I always wanted to do something to help those people."[4] After having his bicycle stolen from him at age twelve, Cassius turned to Louisville policeman Joe Martin for boxing lessons.

Martin said of the young boxer, "He was a kid willing to make the sacrifices necessary to achieve something worthwhile in sports. I realized it was almost impossible to discourage him. He was easily the hardest worker of any kid I ever taught."[5] Commitment and hard work became Clay's childhood response to fear, a reaction that would recur throughout Ali's career and life.

Perhaps the biggest fear of Clay's life came in late 1963 at age twenty-two, when he challenged Sonny Liston for the world heavyweight title. It is difficult to exaggerate how intimidating Liston was at the time; he was considered by many to be the most formidable man in boxing history. Liston had learned to box while serving a term in prison for armed robbery, and was associated with organized crime. Liston was considered the greatest heavyweight boxer of all time. The odds were seven to one in Liston's favor.

Ali set the scene: "Just before the fight, when the referee was giving us instructions, Liston was giving me that stare. And I won't lie; I was scared. Sonny Liston was one of the greatest fighters of all time. He was one of the most scientific boxers who ever lived; he hit hard; and he was fixing to kill me. It frightened me, knowing how hard he hit."[6] In the build-up before the fight, Clay prepared thoroughly, but he also provided entertainment by using self-promotion, demeaning his opponent, and reciting poetry. This behavior was novel; no previous heavyweight boxer had used showmanship to promote the sport.

On February 25, 1964, at the Miami Convention Hall, after six rounds of fighting, Clay "shocked the world" by prevailing against Liston and becoming the world heavyweight champion. Clay had turned fear into courage: "Everyone predicted that Sonny Liston would destroy me. And he was scary. But it's lack of faith that makes people afraid of meeting challenges, and I believed in myself."[7]

AFFIRMATIONS

Clay's use of self-affirmation provided a gift to the world: "It's the repetition of affirmations that leads to belief. And once that belief becomes as deep conviction, things begin to happen."[8] Later in life, Ali said, "I am the greatest, I said that even before I knew I was. I figured that if I said it enough, I would convince the world that I really was the greatest."[9]

A common New Age saying is, "Create Your Own Reality." Ali created his own confidence through "self-talk," or repeated affirmations. Affirmations are simply a conscious effort to control your inner dialogue to alter the way that you think and feel, in order to overcome obstacles and limiting beliefs. This concept of self-talk, or affirmation, is an ancient part of many of the world's religions.

Muhammad Ali, as a practicing Muslim, prayed before each boxing match, and used spiritual self-talk to maintain his confidence. Clay used confidence, affirmation, conviction, and enormous preparation to beat Liston, the scariest heavyweight fighter of the era. Biographer Jonathon Eig reflected on Ali's poise, "He sensed early on that confidence could be a weapon; it made him seem bigger and tougher than he was, and sometimes it rattled opponents."[10]

The transformation of fear into courage had prevailed, and would be replayed throughout Clay's professional and personal life. Eig continues, "Years later, he would admit to friends that he had been frightened before every one of his fights. But he hid it beautifully. And once the bell rang, his fears vanished."[11]

PREPARATION

Muhammad Ali was able to transform fear into courage, transcending anxiety to conquer obstacles. Ali successfully used fear to his advantage as motivation and inspiration for success. Fear became courage. Ali not only transcended fear in the boxing ring, but also, later in life, in social movements. In South Africa, Nelson Mandela devoted his life to securing freedom for people of all races (chapter 8), and discovered the same principle as Ali: "I learned that courage was not the absence of fear, but the triumph over it. . . . The brave man is not he who does not feel afraid, but he who conquers that fear."[12]

What begins as fear about an upcoming lecture, class, or presentation can motivate a teacher into intense preparation, which in turn can result in enhanced performance. Robust presentations occur when the speaker/teacher is confident. Teachers are at their most confident when they are best prepared, and have undertaken the hard work of studying, learning, thinking, evaluating, writing and rewriting, assessing, and reflecting on how their audience will react to every word that they plan to say.

Intense preparation, motivated by fear and anxiety, allows for the transcendence out of fear and into courage. Confidence that comes from knowledge and groundwork transforms fear into courage; changes anxiety to enthusiasm; and provides a unique and productive experience for students and other participants.

PERSONAL CONVICTION

Ali was drafted by the US military in 1967, but refused induction, based on his religious convictions as a member of the Nation of Islam, as well as his assessment of the causes and consequences of the Vietnam War. He believed that the war was based on white supremacy, colonialism, and imperialism. At the time, these views were enormously controversial, and extraordinarily unpopular with most Americans. Perseverance of thought, speech, and action led to a slow realization by the public and the government that Ali's opinions could be correct.

Ali's personal, political, and religious convictions and refusal to be drafted led to a massive negative reaction from the boxing world. He was banned from boxing, his heavyweight title was taken away, his passport was taken away so that he could not fight in other nations, and he was nearly sent to jail as a traitor for standing up against the United States. Ali was banned from his chosen means of making a living for over three years, during 1967–1971. During Ali's exile from boxing, he changed professions from pugilism to public speaking.

PUBLIC SPEAKING

Muhammad Ali wrote and presented lectures at University campuses as a means of supporting himself and his family, when boxing had been taken away from him. Eig reports, "The lectures produced anxiety in Ali, who was insecure about his reading and writing abilities and uncertain what kind of questions he might face from college students. . . . It was painstaking work. For Ali, it was the beginning of a battle to overcome the dyslexia and poor reading skills that had hampered him since childhood."[13]

Ali recalled that, "Putting the lectures together was hard work."[14] He started by writing his ideas on paper, then rewrote the ideas for six speeches on note cards. Ali prepared for his speeches in a manner similar to training for a heavyweight championship bout: practice, repetition, review, and then more practice, repetition, and review. He rehearsed by studying the notecards, then giving the speech to himself and his wife Belinda in front of a mirror. For three months, Ali practiced his speeches, tape recording each speech "so I could hear myself and learn how to improve what I said."[15]

Ali gave 200 speeches, by his count, on topics such as friendship, war, racism, money, and principles. He shared many opinions that his audiences did not agree with, yet the crowds adored him: "All my life, if I wanted to do something I studied those who were good at it; then I memorized what I learned, and believed that I could do it, too. Then I went out and did it."[16] This is powerful advice for a teacher (or anyone) who seeks to do something: study experts; memorize; believe; take action!

In public speaking, as in boxing, Ali's dedication to obsessive practice and rehearsal resulted in an appearance of ease and audience approval. Intense, focused preparation was a large part of Ali's success, both as a boxer and as a lecturer. "I don't count my sit ups. I only start counting when it starts hurting. That is when I start counting, because then it really counts. That's what makes you a champion."[17] Writing and practicing lectures, speeches, classroom presentations, and collaborative activities is perhaps the single most important task of any teacher.

Ali practiced for three months prior to his first speaking engagement; good teachers can reap huge rewards by following Ali's training regimen. "The fight is won or lost far away from the witnesses, behind the lines, in the gym, and out there on the road; long before I dance under those lights."[18] Intense preparation can result in success, particularly early in a teacher's career.

Connecting to an audience can be accomplished using Muhammad Ali's insights into boxing success: showmanship, enormous preparation, and conviction. Willie Nelson, one of country music's most popular performers, shared: "My show is about connecting to the audience. When I walk out onstage, the first thing I do is start searching for a friendly face. Once I make a connection with that person, the energy we've created starts bouncing around to others in the room, and building up so that pretty soon the whole place is lit up like a neon sign."[19]

PERFORMANCE ANXIETY

Willie's summary of a musical concert also captures the teacher's relationship with the interaction of fear and courage. A class begins with trepidation and anxiety, but is transformed into confidence through student energy. Once students begin to enjoy and appreciate the lesson, positive energy is passed back and forth between students and instructor, resulting in a rewarding experience. Education author Parker Palmer says, "I am a teacher at heart, and there are moments in the classroom when I can hardly hold the joy . . . teaching is the finest work I know."[20]

Performance anxiety, or "stage fright," is common among teachers. This is true for both inexperienced and highly experienced teachers. Some experts claim that good teaching requires anxiety; poor performance happens when a teacher is not nervous. A large number of successful individuals have been subject to performance anxiety, including many performers and public personalities, including Mahatma Gandhi, Ella Fitzgerald, Julie Andrews, Adele, and Bob Dylan.

Ali concluded, "Always confront the things you fear. I realized that we are only brave when we have something to lose and we still try. We can't be brave without fear."[21] The paradox of being in a state of simultaneous panic and confidence reflects Ali's idea that bravery not only springs from fear, but is inseparable from fear. This forms the foundation upon which many teaching and life philosophies are built. No risk, no reward. Playing it safe, in teaching as in life, can provide satisfaction, but not the euphoria of taking on a difficult challenge and succeeding.

Ali showed the way: take on meaningful activities that are out of your comfort zone, and use the fear to conquer the task. Success depends on trying new and scary things, leaving the comfort of success by continuously and relentlessly moving on to the next challenge. And, to the extent that success depends on risk-taking behavior, true success depends on and includes failure. No fear; no courage. No failure; no success. That is the way of Ali. "If I let fear stand in my way, I would never have accomplished anything important in my life."[22]

Psychologists suggest that the body's physical response to fear is nearly identical to that of excitement. Anxiety and excitement are both brought on by adrenaline, and result in the "fight or flight response." This response can be a very good thing. When confronted with a frightening task, we can adapt by thinking of the challenge as exciting, rather than fear-invoking. As trite as this sounds ("turn that smile upside down"), it can be a powerful and productive tool.

Individuals who reappraise and reframe anxiety as excitement through self-talk can use fear as an advantage to achieve an Ali-like performance in their work life, and life's work. This method of overcoming fear was used by Muhammad Ali, and is currently employed by high-performing athletes and entertainers: mental visualization; repeated affirmations; and practice, practice, practice. Ali suggests, "To be a great champion you must believe that you are the best. If you're not, pretend you are."[23]

STRATEGIC INTERACTIONS

The study of strategic interactions is a powerful tool to explain many timely, important, and interesting situations and current events in business, international trade and diplomacy, politics, and social interactions. Teachers who think proactively about how their classroom actions and interactions will affect students are following Ali's practice of thinking about his profession in terms of strategic interactions.

Muhammad Ali fought George Foreman in Kinshasa, Zaire (now Democratic Republic of Congo) in the "Rumble in the Jungle" on October 30, 1974. Foreman was the undefeated heavyweight champion of the world, at twenty-five years old, and notorious for hitting hard. Really hard. Ali was an aging thirty-two-year-old, with a reputation for speed, but a four-to-one underdog. Ali had developed a strategy before the fight, later to be named "rope-a-dope." Ali played defense by leaning back against the ropes, and allowing the powerful Foreman to "punch himself out" by hitting Ali repeatedly on the arms and torso.

Ali taunted Foreman continuously and mercilessly, telling Foreman to throw more punches. Foreman did. Ali continued the rope-a-dope strategy until Round Eight, when Foreman became visibly tired. Ali attacked, and knocked the champion down to end the fight. Ali had been hit hundreds of times: arms, body, head. The fight is famous (and infamous) for Ali defeating a younger, stronger Foreman using a strategy that had not been used before.

Foreman summarized the fight: "In boxing, I had a lot of fear. Fear was good. But, for the first time, in the bout with Muhammad Ali, I didn't have any fear. I thought, 'This is easy. This is what I've been waiting for.' No fear at all. No nervousness. And I lost."[24] When fear is absent, the outcome of a performance is jeopardized. Overconfidence, or even an absence of fear, undermines performance and achievement.

Foreman and Ali became close friends after the bout. Foreman says, "[Ali is] the greatest man I've ever known. Not greatest boxer, that's too small for him. He had a gift. He's not pretty, he's beautiful. Everything America should be, Muhammad Ali is."[25]

SHOWMANSHIP

Imitation is a strategy followed by many teachers. Although using others as a guide can be beneficial, care must be taken with such an approach. Ali is a hero to many individuals. Many people attempt to emulate him, without success. Many teachers strive to become like other outstanding teachers, but this strategy is fraught. People are enormously, incomprehensibly, and wonderfully diverse. To be ultimately successful in all of our pursuits, we must be authentic.

Showmanship is part of teaching, although most teachers would prefer not to admit that lectures or presentations are a performance. Muhammad Ali was the champion of showmanship: bragging, taunting, reciting poetry, being audacious. Ali claimed that the origin of his behavior was professional wrestler Gorgeous George. As a young boxer, Ali shared a radio show with George, learning how "self-promotion and colorful controversy could draw in the crowds."[26]

George's egotistical ranting, outrageous claims, and flamboyant behavior caused a young Clay to want to see the next Gorgeous George match: "I didn't care if he won or lost. I just wanted to be there to see what happened. Me, and a thousand other people. . . . And I thought to myself, all these people are here to see this guy get beat. They all paid to get in. And I said to myself, this is a good idea."[27] George also inspired musical performers James Brown and Bob Dylan with flamboyance, controversy, and taunting the audience.

Provoking the audience is a method of enhancing ticket sales in wrestling and boxing, as well as an advanced speaking technique. Speaking the truth to an audience, even if the truth is not what they want to hear, can generate a high level of intrigue. During his University lectures, Ali shared his views on the Vietnam War, racism, black pride, hatred, homosexuality, the Nation of Islam, and poverty. Ali had enough strong, diverse opinions to make everyone in the audiences disagree with him about at least one, and probably more, issues.

During his exile from boxing, Muhammad Ali not only put his career on the line but also stood strong in the face of government intrusion into his life. Each of his public appearances was closely monitored and recorded by the US government. Ali had done what very few have the courage to do: speak truth to power. Teachers who share sincerity, truth, and conviction with students will always have a special place in our society, and in the heart of their students.

DYNAMICS

A musical metaphor for the teaching dualities of fear/courage, kindness/ rigor, and comfort/afflict comes from grunge rock: Nirvana, Pearl Jam, and Audioslave. Many songs written and performed by these groups follow the "soft/loud" pattern, where the verses are quiet (*piano*) and the chorus is loud and harsh (*forte*): a musical version of floating like a butterfly and stinging like a bee. Nirvana's "Smells like Teen Spirit" comes to mind. This use of musical "dynamics" reflects a long history in all types and genres of music, stage, and literature to build tension, then release.

Dynamics are used to create a contrast between restrained verses and loud and harsh choruses, similar to winning over an audience with kindness, sincerity, honesty, then use the rapport to challenge with a strong truth or opposing viewpoint. The pervasive use of this form of musical dynamics provides evidence for the success of teaching with Ali-style duality: contrast information that is agreeable and straightforward with more challenging material that may provoke and afflict.

Good teachers can build tension to engage students, then create a release to provide satisfaction and a pleasurable liberation from the strain. Together, tension and release make good music . . . and good lectures!

Ali was widely recognized for his enormous philanthropy, good deeds, and public service. He devoted millions to charitable organizations and people in need of all religious backgrounds. It is estimated that Ali helped to feed over 22 million hungry people globally.[28] Ali was recruited to serve on diplomatic missions as an ambassador of peace by the United States. Ali's generosity and sincere assistance to others is unprecedented, and he was in financial difficulty throughout his life, due in part to enormous contributions to people in need.

One of Ali's greatest assets was his ability to endure punishment in the ring. Ali could take devastating blows and remain upright and fighting. He asked his sparring opponents to hit him at full force to prepare for his fights. Ali's toughness may be the cause of his 1984 diagnosis with Parkinson's syndrome. Sadly and ironically, this disease gradually eroded Ali's abilities to move and speak, the two activities that brought Ali widespread success.

With characteristic courage and grace, Ali accepted his changing capabilities. "Change is an inevitable part of life. The seasons change, our feelings change, our appearance will change, and our health will change. Life is easier when we accept these changes and recognize how every moment of our journey is an important part of the growth of our soul."[29] Ali spent less time in the public spotlight, and more time with his family.

IMPERFECT HERO; IMPERFECT TEACHERS

Muhammad Ali was not a perfect person. Ali did not treat some of his wives well. His enormous verbal talent was at times mean-spirited and racist, homophobic, and sexist. No heroes are perfect; no teachers are perfect. As humans, teachers often have a strong desire for heroes, parents, teachers, and friends to be flawless. As teachers experience life, and make classroom mistakes, they no longer desire immaculate heroes.

In many ways, Ali was characterized by competing ideas. Ali was a prize fighter, but a man of peace, who shared the peace of Islam and anti-war sentiment throughout the world. Ali was considered to be enormously kind, but used verbal taunts, freestyle poetry, and songs to intimidate and make fun of his opponents. This duality is consistent with the work of a teacher. Instructors are motivated by the high ideals of helping students learn. Yet, teachers fall short of this ideal every day, subject to human weakness: emotion, limited knowledge, gaps in empathy.

Teachers strongly identify with Ali's conflicted personality, imperfections, and failures. Teaching requires taking risks, adopting new ideas, trying new assessment techniques, and including new pedagogical strategies. Not all newly introduced content or strategies work well. In many cases, a teacher will prepare a lecture, assignment, or exam that worked well in the previous semester or term, referring to good feedback from students, both verbal and nonverbal, or solid performance. This preparation can lead to unanticipated challenges, or even epic failure.

What worked well once does not necessarily work well again. Good teaching requires flexibility and nimbleness to recover from inevitable setbacks, and move forward. A single lecture will often have numerous small failures, noticed by both students and teachers. The audacity of Ali helps teachers move forward in a continuous cycle of improvement, corrections, and growth. A good sense of humor can make almost anything that happens in the classroom acceptable. And, being sincere can refocus student attention on the subject matter.

CONCLUSION

The main take-home message from Muhammad Ali is to use fear and/or anxiety to your advantage. Ali stated, "If your dreams don't scare you, they aren't big enough."[30] Teachers take risks. By definition, these risks will work sometimes, and lead to failure in other cases. Take risks anyway. One of the definitions of "leverage" is to use something to maximum advantage. Leverage your fear for a great performance!

Ali used unrelenting dedication to prepare for his tasks, both fights and lectures: "Early in my career I learned to run until I was tired, then run even more after that. But all the running I did before the fatigue and pain was just the introduction to my workout. The real conditioning began when the pain set in. That was when it was time to start pushing. That was when I would count every mile as extra strength and stamina." Ali continued, "What counts in the ring is what you can do after you're exhausted. The same is true of life."[31] Preparation at this high level led to the appearance of ease, both in the boxing ring and in the lecture hall.

Ali had a strong desire to succeed. This is a core value that can be encouraged, nourished, and grown in both students and teachers. Bob Dylan wrote, "[Ali] instilled courage and fear in the hearts of men, and remains a firelight of strength and independence. He proved that you can stand up for your beliefs in the face of adversity and still remain standing."[32] Ali's view of life was based on fear and courage. Late in life, facing physical challenges, he wrote: "All through my life, I have been tested. My will has been tested, my courage has been tested, my strength has been tested. Now my patience and endurance are being tested."[33]

Teachers who face performance anxiety as they prepare for class need not recoil from the fear. Instead, they can embrace the angst by recognizing that the source of the anxiety is excitement and enthusiasm for the opportunity to practice their craft, to provide positive affirmation to their students, and to share their version of the truth with others.

Teachers who have never overcome fear, even after years of teaching, can view fear as a main feature of their teaching career, and view it as a gift. Embraced anxiety is a catalyst for enhanced performance. Strive to maintain positive energy in the face of doubt, fear, and anxiety. Dive headfirst into fear on purpose, to use fear for a purpose. With every lecture, speech, and classroom presentation, teachers can leverage their anxiety/enthusiasm to make the world a better place. For this, they can be grateful to the boxer who used fear to change the world, The Greatest of All Time.

INTERSECTIONS

If the measure of greatness is to gladden the heart of every human being on the face of the earth, then he truly was the greatest. In every way he was the bravest, kindest, and most excellent of men.

—Bob Dylan, on Muhammad Ali.[34]

TEACHING SUMMARY: LECTURE LIKE ALI

- Preparation. Enormous preparation and dedication result in success. Plan, prepare, practice, repeat. Think of Ali preparing for a fight: repetition, affirmation, and dedication. Think of Ali preparing for his lectures: repetition, affirmation, and dedication.
- Affirmations. Create your own confidence through self-talk. "I am good at this." "I will inspire my students today." "This will be a great lecture." Repeat positive thoughts and feelings. Share repeated affirmations with students, colleagues, family members, and strangers. This is the way of Ali.
- Fear. Use fear and anxiety to leverage success. If you aren't scared, expand your goals.
- Audacity. Use a little bit of Gorgeous George in your performances, lectures, and behavior. Be outrageous! Or at least a little provocative.
- Conviction. Be yourself. Be true to yourself. Share your truth and convictions. Be your best self. Every time. All the time.

NOTES

1. Eig, *Ali*, 115.
2. Eig, *Ali*, 530.
3. *Observer*, 9.
4. Parks, "Redemption."
5. Lipsyte, "Free to Be," 11.
6. Hauser, *Life and Times*, 74.
7. Hauser, *Life and Times*, 60.
8. Johnson, "Muhammad Ali."
9. Telegraph Sport, "30 Best Quotes."
10. Eig, *Ali*, 38.
11. Eig, *Ali*, 44.
12. Mandela, *Long Walk*, 622.
13. Eig, *Ali*, 259.
14. Hauser, *Life and Times*, 185.
15. Hauser, *Life and Times*, 185.
16. Ali and Ali, *Butterfly*, 204.
17. Spio, "Rocket Science," 115.
18. Rovell, "Best Quotes."
19. Nelson, *Tao*, 52.
20. Palmer, *Courage*, 1.
21. Ali and Ali, *Butterfly*, 28.
22. Ali and Ali, *Butterfly*, 28.
23. Santiago, "Leadership Quotes."
24. Rajpal, "Foreman."

25. Zirin, "Foreman."
26. Ali and Ali, *Butterfly*, 71.
27. Ali and Ali, *Butterfly*, 71–72.
28. Christopher and Smith, *Sports Heroes*.
29. Ali and Ali, *Butterfly*, 146.
30. WonderfulQuote.com, "Muhammad Ali."
31. Ali and Ali, *Butterfly*, 130.
32. Hauser, *Life and Times*, 507.
33. Ali and Ali, *Butterfly*, xix.
34. Dylan, "Muhammad Ali."

REFERENCES

Ali, Muhammad, and Hana Yasmeen Ali. *The Soul of a Butterfly: Reflections on Life's Journey*. New York: Simon & Shuster, 2004.

Christopher, Paul J. and Alicia Marie Smith. *Greatest Sports Heroes of All Time: North American Edition*. Evanston, IL: Encouragement Press, 2006.

Dylan, Bob. "Bob Dylan on Muhammad Ali." June 4, 2016. Accessed August 17, 2018. https://www.bobdylan.com/news/bob-dylan-muhammad-ali/

Eig, Jonathon. *Ali: A Life*. Boston, MA: Houghton Mifflin Harcourt, 2017.

Hauser, Thomas. *Muhammad Ali: His Life and Times*. New York: Simon & Schuster, 1991.

Johnson, Jeff. "Muhammad Ali In His Own Words: Six of His Best Quotes to Live By." *NBC News*, June 4, 2016. https://www.nbcnews.com/news/nbcblk/remembering-muhammad-ali-six-quotes-pack-punch-n585571

Lipsyte, Robert. "Free to Be Muhammad Ali." *Sports Illustrated*, September 25, 1961.

Mandela, Nelson. *Long Walk to Freedom: The Autobiography of Nelson Mandela*. New York: Holt, Rinehart, and Winston, 2000.

Nelson, Willie, with Turk Pipkin. *The Tao of Willie: A Guide to the Happiness in Your Heart*. New York: Gotham, 2006.

Observer, London. Sunday, December 19, 1971, page 9.

Palmer, Parker. *The Courage to Teach. Exploring the Inner Landscape of a Teacher's Life*. San Francisco, CA: Jossey-Bass, 1998.

Parks, Gordon. "The Redemption of the Champion." *Life*, September 9, 1966.

Rajpal, Monita. "Interview with George Foreman." *CNN Transcript*, April 26, 2013. http://edition.cnn.com/TRANSCRIPTS/1304/26/ta.01.html

Rovell, Darren. "Muhammad Ali's 10 Best Quotes." *ESPN*, June 6, 2016. https://www.espn.com/boxing/story/_/id/15930888/muhammad-ali-10-best-quotes

Santiago, José. "12 Inspiring Leadership Quotes from Muhammad Ali." *World Economic Forum*, 2016. https://www.weforum.org/agenda/2016/06/12-leadership-quotes-from-muhammad-ali/

Spio, Mary. *It's Not Rocket Science: 7 Game-Changing Traits for Uncommon Success*. London: Penguin, 2016.

Telegraph Sport. "Muhammad Ali: 30 Best Quotes from the Heavyweight Champion." Accessed August 2, 2021. https://www.telegraph.co.uk/news/2016/06/04/muhammad-ali-30-best-quotes-from-the-heavyweight-champion/

WondefulQuote.com. "Muhammad Ali: A Collection of the Best Muhammad Ali Quotes." Accessed August 9, 2018. https://www.wonderfulquote.com/a/muhammad-ali-quotes

Zirin, Dave. "An Interview with George Foreman." *Counterpunch.org*, November 7, 2003. https://www.counterpunch.org/2003/11/07/an-interview-with-george-foreman/

Chapter 2

Salvation from Stagnation

Bob Dylan

Figure 2.1 **Bob Dylan.** *Source*: Wikimedia Commons. National Archives and Records Administration, National Archives Identifier (NAID) 542021.

The highest purpose of art is to inspire.

—Bob Dylan[1]

All I can do is be me, whoever that is.

—Bob Dylan[2]

CHAPTER SYNOPSIS

Bob Dylan's constant makeovers and genre changes provide inspiration for teachers to continuously adopt new methods, take on new challenges, and remain enthusiastic about student learning throughout their careers. Two characteristics of Dylan's success are explored: (1) his huge early investment in the mastery of music, and (2) his style of borrowing ideas from great music. Like Bob Dylan, teachers can find success by mastering their subject matter early, and mimicking the teaching practices of outstanding educators.

Bob Dylan performed at the Midland Theater in Kansas City in October 2019 to an appreciative intergenerational crowd. The show was extraordinary. Dylan played an eclectic mix of songs, some old, some new, all excellent. At different times during the course of the evening, Dylan played electric guitar, harmonica, keyboards, and an old upright piano positioned in the middle of the stage.

The performance was inspired and innovative: the songs were all performed differently than the recorded versions. Changing how songs are performed is a Bob Dylan trademark, and even the most devoted fans must listen carefully to discern which song was being played. Although the songs were from a wide variety of musical genres (blues, folk, rock, gospel), the lyrics seemed relevant and timely, including: "It's Not Dark Yet, but It's Getting There."

Most, but not all, of the audience was completely mesmerized with the energy, enthusiasm, and force of the performance. The assembled crowd included college students and elderly men; and some middle-aged daughters taking their fathers or parents to see Bob Dylan. Some audience members were giddy with excitement, others had been drinking heavily, some were angry with the ushers who strictly enforced the no-late arrivals and no-photos policies.

Some danced, some smiled, some sang along to the extent possible, because Bob will fool you with the tempo, timing, and delivery of the lyrics. How was it possible for a seventy-eight-year-old to command the room? What can be learned from Bob Dylan's exceptional and long career? How could a teacher use Dylan's unique ability to transform a classroom into a memorable, motivational, and meaningful experience? Perhaps Dylan's magic and mystique could be identified and transferred to educational settings.

Bob Dylan has been widely regarded as a virtuoso songwriter and prolific recording artist for over five decades. He is known for relentless, continuous transformation across genres and musical styles. His career trajectory is fascinating, unique, and highly successful, resulting in numerous awards recognizing his contributions to music and songwriting. Dylan's performance style is unique; many listeners find his voice and arrangements unappealing or even unsettling.

Philosopher Theodore Gracyk refers to this as Dylan's "aesthetic of imperfection."[3] Throughout his career, Dylan has challenged his audience with new versions of well-known songs, performed in ways that make them hard to recognize, and easy for some to dislike. Fans often have to work to figure out what song is being performed, resulting in a disconnect between past knowledge and new experience that keeps listeners active and interested.

Dylan's continuous makeovers have allowed him to maintain enormous creativity and productivity over time. He has produced thirty-nine albums in a wide range of genres and styles: folk, blues, country, gospel, rock and roll, rockabilly, English, Scottish, and Irish folk music, jazz, and Americana. His lyrics incorporate literature, philosophy, religious references, political influences, and a great deal more. In 2017, he was awarded the Nobel Prize in Literature. His style is both original, and ever-changing. There is no one else like Bob Dylan, and his career provides potent and pragmatic lessons for teaching and learning.

CONTINUOUS CHANGE

Innovation provides higher levels of interest and fun. Students can get tired or bored with the same ideas, formats, and routines. The implication for teaching is that change can be powerful pedagogical tool. Do something different during a lecture. Something as simple as walking to the far side of the classroom, and lecturing from there. Students are often most attentive when teachers do something unexpected. Changing the assignments can also create a new experience that can be positively experienced by a class. Many small changes, quirks, and unanticipated statements can provide a catalyst for learning.

This is where Bob Dylan is truly masterful. Not only does Dylan change genres frequently, but he also changes nearly everything about his performances often; always; forever. Dylan also changes his background story, and his own identity. The movie *I'm Not There* is a creative biography inspired by the life of Bob Dylan.[4] Six different actors depict different stories taken from Dylan's life: poet, prophet, outlaw, born-again Christian, folk musician, and rock star.

Educators can adopt a Dylanesque strategy by continuously revamping, revising, rewriting, and rethinking lectures, classes, assignments, exams, requirements, and classroom personas. Successful teachers, entertainers, comedians, parents, politicians, and people in sales all focus on one simple feature of their efforts: what works best.

Teachers can adopt numerous pedagogical strategies over a decades-long attempt to provide useful knowledge to students: flipped classroom, collaborative learning, team assignments, team exams, team reports, daily quizzes, multiple choice exams, essay exams, comedic interjections, life-skill anecdotes, personal stories, sermon-like lectures, blackboards with white chalk, white boards with black ink, overhead projectors, PowerPoint slides, bells and whistles, oral exams, stern lectures, kind lectures, and courses with discussions and papers. Small classes, large classes, required classes, and elective classes.

Continuous change provides many positive outcomes. It keeps students from boredom. It reduces the possibility of stagnation. Try something new! The rush of nerves that comes from introducing something new into a class provides the "edge" of fear and adrenaline that produces something special. This is the magic of Bob Dylan. Change everything possible: tone, beat, measure, style, genre, and you will hit on something transcendent.

MAKING STRANGE

Dylan also changes his singing enormously: phrasing, rhythm, pitch, articulation, and timbre. Writers and artists call this type of change, "defamiliarization," an artistic technique of using language in a way that makes ordinary objects appear differently. Teachers can usefully take familiar concepts, ideas, and objects, and purposefully "make them strange." Art, and teaching, can make the routine strange, the mundane exhilarating, and allow students to see old things in a new way.

Familiarity can lead to habituation and stagnation. Defamiliarization keeps students and teachers alive, awake, and alert. This creative tension between old and new ideas forms an effective model of student learning.[5]

Three of Dylan's major changes include (1) abandonment of his folk fan base in 1966 by switching from acoustic to electric guitar in a shift from folk to rock music, (2) conversion to Christianity (1978), resulting in gospel songwriting and performances, and (3) a recommitment to performing (1987), with the beginning of the "Never Ending Tour." Dylan has appeared in over 100 concerts per year during 1987–2019.

Many teachers are concerned about adopting a new pedagogical technique, such as a flipped classroom format, daily quizzes, or collaborative learning. In many cases, new practices can be attempted in a trial format. Teachers unsure of any classroom innovation can gain confidence by trying new ideas in small, less risky trials: try out a new idea in a single lecture.

Teachers are often at their best in the college classroom when trying out a new pedagogical technique, discussing a new topic, or presenting information that is new to them. The strong desire to "make it work" (*intention*), combined with freshness of approach (*inspiration*), results in superior teaching efforts. Bob Dylan's restless, ubiquitous, unrelenting makeovers of himself, his genre, his performance style, and his songs provide a catalyst to greater musical experiences, and enhanced fascination with his performances. Fans wonder what he will do next. Dylan combats routine and stagnation by change.

In 2009, Dylan performed a new release, "Forgetful Heart" in a live concert. For most of the concert, he played keyboards. About midway through the performance, Dylan emerged from behind the console, and positioned himself at the front and center of the stage, inches from the audience. His body language, facial expression, and tension made his discomfort clear.

Nevertheless, he persisted, making the song the highlight of the evening. The song's immediacy, painful self-disclosure, and unique performance style with a vintage, hand-held microphone led to a unique and unforgettable vocal performance. It is enlightening to realize that one of the most successful performers of all time forces himself out of his comfort zone, makes himself nervous, perhaps even scared, to provide a stunning, memorable performance. Teachers can do this, too.

Changes in teaching are often challenging, since the status quo provides assurance that comes from experience. Change saves us from becoming bored and stagnant, but often requires a stress-induced transition from old to new practices. Excellent teachers retain the best characteristics of old content, tools, and pedagogies, while simultaneously adopting new teaching practices and content. Like Bob Dylan, engaged teachers use *intention* to provide the most useful, important, and timely material possible, combined with *inspiration* to use new approaches to make the classroom environment memorable and enthusiastic.

Continuous adoption of new technology and classroom strategy can result in a positive classroom environment. Trying something new provides a burst of adrenaline. The risk that a new approach might not work results in an edge of tension that translates into teaching effectiveness. Continuous change, coupled with assessment and improvement, can become a solid foundation for always seeking more effective teaching and learning.

PEDAGOGICAL TRIAGE

Change is among the most powerful ideas for improved teaching: try something new, and make it work. Keep the positive features and eliminate any negative elements. This strategy could be called "pedagogical triage." The idea is for teachers to prioritize projects or activities based on the promotion of student learning. Once the priority list is completed, teachers can enhance successful strategies, and reduce or eliminate unsuccessful pedagogies. Continuous improvement in teaching occurs through continuous movement out of less successful strategies and into more productive approaches.

AUTHENTIC TEACHERS

Dylan's songs are enormously complex, layered with nuance, ambiguity, and metaphor. His music sounds simultaneously new and old, and the meaning is purposefully vague, and left up to the listener. Like the work of many great artists, the listener can project his or her own feelings, experiences, and attitudes onto the artist's work. This makes Bob Dylan among the greatest songwriters of all time, and truly iconic, incomprehensible, and worthy of imitation. Dylan combines strong *intention* with *inspiration*: intention to share his ideas in music and lyrics; inspiration to provide meaning through new ways of performing his songs.

Dylan's life, religion, and contribution are embedded in his music, and inseparable from his songs. Dylan has always followed his own desires, rather than do what others expect, want, or need. This has led to controversy, conflict, and strong emotions by fans who often feel rejected as Dylan transitions between styles.

Dylan has an important lesson for teachers. Not just important, but perhaps the single most important lesson: to be the best teacher possible, be your authentic self. Whoever that is. Dylan trusted himself more than anyone else, including managers, fans, and other recording artists, followed his destiny, and became the greatest songwriter of all time. Many teachers worry that they don't have enough charisma, intelligence, knowledge, charm, popularity, or humor to be an outstanding teacher. However, any educator, of any personality type, temperament, or perceived intelligence level can be an outstanding teacher.

Teachers who combine strong intentions with inspiration can provide great learning experiences for their students. Education author Parker Palmer states that it is "impossible to claim that all good teachers use similar techniques: some lecture non-stop and others speak very little, some stay close to their material and others loose the imagination, some teach with the carrot and others with the stick."[6]

Personal styles, strategies, and classroom techniques alone are not the key to teaching success. Bob Dylan captures the key to success with a simple, short phrase in his Nobel lecture: "I hope what I say will be worthwhile and purposeful."[7] Dylan used the lecture to describe books that were meaningful and inspirational to him.

New Yorker writer Alexandra Schwartz summarized the lecture: "[Dylan] is totally immersed not only in what he had read but in his memory of it; the books are alive in him, and as he talks about them we, too, begin to see them afresh. What sets great writers apart from the pack is their ability to connect with readers on a visual level. We feel their work in our brains and in our guts."[8] In this sense, good teaching can be Dylanesque.

Good teachers are authentic; genuine; sincere. The best teachers bring their authentic self to class, share their actual person with students, and desire to improve the lives of others by sincerely sharing themselves and their knowledge with students. Like Bob Dylan's diverse styles, a wide diversity of individuals can teach, and teach effectively. Dylan used desire, intensity, purposefulness, confidence, and charisma. The strong desire to do well, paired with tenacity, result in positive outcomes in any endeavor. The desire to succeed provides the most important ingredient to success in any endeavor, including teaching.

EXTENSIVE PREPARATION

Good teachers use any strategy that helps students learn. Excellent educators work at the best of their ability as a teacher, and prompt students to perform at the best of their ability, too. These teachers do not make the course material unnecessarily difficult or intimidating. Instead, they clarify, explain, motivate, champion, exalt, and teach in a consistently upbeat attitude. A teacher's optimism is selflessly shared; deep enthusiasm for the course is obvious.

Effective teachers cheerfully and professionally share their love for their subject, their jobs, and their students. Years later, much of the content is retained from classes, lectures, and courses taught in a "student-friendly," non-threatening environment. An experienced teacher's friendliness and desire to help students typically comes from a place of confidence. Teachers who know the material well can be friendly, casual, and authoritative. A solid learning environment is generated through modest self-confidence, solid preparation, and a deep knowledge of the course material.

One of the best ways to overcome performance anxiety is to prepare so well that the nervousness becomes excitement (chapter 1). Bob Dylan described his own career in his Nobel Lecture as one of deep knowledge of music, which led to excellence. Dylan learned how to write songs by immersing himself in old songs, building upon the knowledge of what had come before.

As a teenager, Dylan was obsessed with Woody Guthrie's folk music, and devoted his early career to intense, robust, exhaustive study of Guthrie's music, and folk music in general. For an aspiring artist, this investment proved to be exceptionally productive. His early mastery of folk music allowed him to be successful for the rest of his career.

Beginning teachers can effectively mirror Dylan's early investment. Early investment in mastery of content, teaching methods, and student needs is among the most effective strategies of successful teaching. Devoting a great deal of time and energy to learning the fundamentals of our craft allows teachers to build expertise in a cumulative fashion. In economic jargon, investments in human capital by teachers yield a compound rate of return. The sooner the investment in knowledge occurs and the greater the effort at mastery, the higher the payoff will be over the teacher's lifetime.

One effective practice for teaching a course for the first time is to devote extra effort and care to develop the course materials and learn the content in a deep, immersive fashion. Teach like Dylan: master your craft and content early and well.

INTERTEXTUALITY

Dylan's liberal use of other people's ideas can provide a source of confidence for teachers. Dylan confessed to his talent scout and record producer John Hammond, "Some stuff I've written, some stuff I've discovered, some stuff I stole."[9] Good teachers are careful and vigilant to share with students the importance of plagiarism and cheating. Claiming others' ideas as your own is unacceptable. This concern for truth and accuracy is right and just. However, using other people's ideas, thoughts, and concepts to enhance your own work is a necessary ingredient to teaching success.

After all, content that is taught came from a previous teacher, often a textbook or other source of knowledge. Dylan's confession that he "stole" some material refers to the concept of "intertextuality," a process used by artists, writers, and speakers to produce new meaning through the creative reuse of existing texts, images, or sounds. Intertextuality is one major ingredient of Dylan's magic, complexity, and enduring success. It is odd to speak of authenticity and using others' ideas simultaneously, but this defines Dylan's enormous contribution.

When listeners are first exposed to Bob Dylan, they are often drawn in to the unusual music, unique vocal style, and poetic lyrics. It can be difficult to articulate or explain interest in Dylan, and the continuing desire to listen to his music. Dylan's music sounds both old and new. The songs are often recorded in an enjoyable style: blues, country, rockabilly, gospel.

Yet, the songs do not follow the same pattern as the genres' predecessors; the music is also new. The lyrics are enormously evocative. The words cause listeners to recall their past, reflect on their present, and wonder about their future, including remembrances of joyful youth, life's challenges, places lived, situations encountered, and relationships. Dylan explains, "Folk songs were the way that I explored the universe, they were pictures and the pictures were worth more than anything I could say. I knew the inner substance of the thing."[10]

Dylan's use of previous lyrics and ideas causes listeners to recall the context of the reused item, catalyzing a cornucopia of thoughts, memories, and new ideas. Richard F. Thomas explains: "this is how literature works, and it is how Dylan's song works when it takes on the songs and texts that are in his tradition. . . . Dylan is in a tradition that is old and his connecting to those traditions is a big part of what his art is about."[11] Many of Dylan's greatest hits are closely based on and reactions to previous songs; including songs by Woody Guthrie, John Lennon, gospel standards, blues, and jazz.

Dylan's intertextuality provides a path for continuous improvement: recall your favorite teacher and use him or her as a role model for teaching and learning. When teachers are at their best, explanations and examples, empathy for students, teaching style, and enthusiasm for the material are all taken, or borrowed, from their own teachers!

CONCLUSION

Before each semester, teachers can effectively modify and update courses to strive for growth and improvement. The use of pedagogical triage, with intention and inspiration, can move a course forward. At times, some teachers move quickly, and adopt new teaching practices, methodologies, and course content that take them out of their comfort zone. Other times, teachers can feel reluctant to drop a course component that has been used successfully for many years, but could usefully be dropped or modified. Most often, it is incremental changes that are undertaken each semester that lead to the best outcomes.

Inspiration causes excitement and enthusiasm for the implementation of new ideas. Intention provides the steady desire to base a course on a solid foundation of best pedagogical practices, up-to-date course content, and instructor integrity. Together, inspiration and intention can provide maximal performance outcomes. Teach like Bob Dylan by combining the old with the new through a creative process of change and improvement.

Not every idea will work. Do it anyway! Improvement can occur through quick success, but it is more likely to come from failure. Most inspirations in teaching and learning combine elements of both success and failure (this idea is further explored with Fred Rogers in chapter 3). The careful, intentional teacher will move forward embellishing the successful components of the course and minimizing, modifying, or eliminating the less-than-successful course features.

Teach like Bob Dylan: be simultaneously complex and simple; clear and unclear; new and old, genuine and a copycat. In a career trajectory of extensive preparation, pedagogical triage, continuous change, and defamiliarization, an effective teacher will not stop at the level of her role models. Instead, the successful teacher will transcend the predecessors and antecedents using their unique individual talents in a complex, inexplicable, unknowable way, and create a superior learning environment for students.

One final characteristic deserves study and reflection: the mystery, magic, and enigma of Bob Dylan. Teachers with an authentic sense of charisma or mystique provide a curious allure to students. One certainly does not have to be as aloof and unknowable as Bob Dylan to be a successful teacher, speaker, or performer. But a strong conviction for continuous improvement through intertextuality, or borrowing the magnetism of other teachers, can provide a certain atmosphere of mystery that causes students to lean in and pay attention.

Dylan's lyrics are commonly seen as opaque, mysterious, and difficult to understand. What do they mean? Dylan answered this question in his 2017 Nobel speech: "If a song moves you, that's all that's important."[12] This statement is a simple distillation of all that matters to motivate a teacher and console anxiety about upcoming lectures and courses. If a teacher sticks with what moves her, stays true to herself, and shares her authentic self, then she has done all that she can. And that is enough. Be yourself, by borrowing the most effective ideas, techniques, and strategies from the best of the best. Then make them your own.

INTERSECTIONS

I looked up from the podium and I thought to myself, "I've never seen such a large crowd." I was up close when King was giving that speech. To this day, it still affects me in a profound way.

—Bob Dylan on Martin Luther King Jr.'s "I Have a Dream" speech at the 1963 March on Washington. Dylan performed his song, "Only a Pawn in Their Game" immediately before King's speech.[13]

TEACHING SUMMARY: PERFORM LIKE BOB DYLAN

- Continuous change; pedagogical triage; creative destruction.
- Be weird and mysterious. But not too much.
- Investment. Work hard at learning the fundamentals of your subject matter. The sooner the investment, the larger the payoff.
- Try new pedagogical styles in small trials. Base incremental changes on sound practices and content.
- "Defamiliarize" the material by presenting common ideas and concepts in an unfamiliar way to enhance perception of the familiar.
- Intertextuality. Borrow the best examples, material, methods, and style from your best teachers.
- First, invest in becoming as good as your role models. Then, transcend them and be even better than your role models!

NOTES

1. Cott, "Interview."
2. Dylan, "Interview."
3. Gracyk, "Masterpiece."
4. Haynes, "Not There."
5. Barkley and Coffey, "Student Learning."
6. Palmer, "Teacher," 2.
7. Dylan, *Nobel Lecture*, 1.
8. Schwartz, "Nobel Speech."
9. Heylin, *Bob Dylan*, 8.
10. Dylan, *Chronicles*, 18.
11. Thomas, *Dylan Matters*, 133.
12. Dylan, *Nobel Lecture*, 22.
13. Scorsese, *No Direction Home*.

REFERENCES

Barkley, Andrew, and Brian K. Coffey. "An Economic Model of Student Learning." *Journal of Agricultural and Applied Economics* 50, no. 4 (November 2018): 1–23. doi: 10.1017/aae.2018.13.

Cott, Jonathan. "Bob Dylan: The Rolling Stone Interview." *Rolling Stone*, January 26, 1978.

Dylan, Bob. *Chronicles*, Volume One. New York: Simon & Schuster. 2004.

Dylan, Bob. "Interview with Bob Dylan." *In-Beat Magazine*, May 1965. https://ilove-muggsy.tripod.com/BobDylan/id12.html

Dylan, Bob. *The Nobel Lecture*. New York: Simon & Schuster, 2017.

Gracyk, Theodore. "When I Paint My Masterpiece: What Sort of Artist is Bob Dylan?" In *Bob Dylan and Philosophy: It's Alright, Ma (I'm Only Thinking)*, eds. Peter Vernezze and Carl J. Porter, 169–81. Chicago: Open Court, 2006.

Haynes, Todd, Dir. *I'm Not There*. Perfs. Christian Bale, Cate Blanchett, Marcus Carl Franklin, Richard Gere, Heath Ledger. 2007, New York: The Weinstein Company, 2007. Film.

Heylin, C. *Bob Dylan: The Recording Sessions 1960-94*. New York: St. Martin's Griffin, 1996.

Palmer, Parker J. "The Heart of a Teacher: Identity and Integrity in Teaching." *Change: The Magazine of Higher Learning* 29, no. 6 (November, 1997): 14–21. doi: 10.1080/00091389709602343.

Schwartz, Alexandra. "The Rambling Glory of Bob Dylan's Nobel Speech." *The New Yorker*, June 6. 2017. https://www.newyorker.com/culture/culture-desk/the-rambling-glory-of-bob-dylans-nobel-speech

Scorsese, Martin, Dir. *No Direction Home*. Perf. Bob Dylan. 2005, Los Angeles, CA: Paramount Pictures, 2005. Documentary film.

Thomas, Richard F. *Why Bob Dylan Matters*. New York: HarperCollins, 2017.

Chapter 3

Success from Failure

Mister Rogers

Figure 3.1 Fred Rogers. *Source*: Wikimedia Commons. Walt Seng.

Anyone who does anything to help a child in his life is a hero to me.

—Fred Rogers[1]

There are three ways to ultimate success: the first way is to be kind. The second way is to be kind. The third way is to be kind.

—Fred Rogers[2]

CHAPTER SYNOPSIS

Teachers face numerous and diverse challenges. Mister Rogers is an extraordinary role model for effective teaching and learning. Mister Rogers provides teachers with the comfort of knowing that one cannot teach without making mistakes. He also shows educators how to successfully use mistakes, human errors, and failure to learn, improve, and grow. This is powerful knowledge. A failure in performance faced by rock icon Patti Smith is described and analyzed to enhance teachers' ability to overcome failure.

Mister Rogers asserted that effective teaching is based on kindness. He was not wrong. A teacher's knowledge of kindness grows with experience, allowing for greater effectiveness over time. However, the path is not always smooth, and is at times subject to failure, mistakes, and obstacles. Fred Rogers provides the needed balm: when in doubt, read some quotes from Mister Rogers, or better yet, watch an episode or two of *Mister Rogers' Neighborhood*. Teachers who pay careful attention to Rogers' methods will be rewarded, inspired, and refreshed.

Fred Rogers used kindness to dramatically change children's television, and the world. The PBS show *Mister Rogers' Neighborhood* combined state-of-the-art broadcast technology with deeply held ethical values: kindness, respect, understanding, tolerance, and inclusion. The show reached a nationwide audience of millions of viewers for 865 episodes, from 1968 to 2001. Rogers' creative, soothing blend of fantasy and reality captivated children with a deliberate, slow pace and quiet manner. The show enjoyed enormous success due simply to an adult speaking kindly and directly to each child in the viewing audience.

Rogers offered unconditional love and acceptance to all preschool children. Viewers were completely engaged for the entire thirty-minute episodes, which all started with the signature song, "Won't You Be My Neighbor." Rogers' uncompromising determination led to shows of the highest standards, intended to educate children about their feelings, emotions, and relationships. The shows included music, special guests, skits, puppetry, and gently communicated solutions to common everyday challenges such as tying shoelaces, making friends, and mailing a letter.

Rogers nicely and confidently shared enormous empathy, without regard to how critics may have viewed him. Musician Wynton Marsalis, a guest on *Mister Rogers' Neighborhood* declared, "Fred Rogers was one of a kind—an American original . . . there was no one like him. . . . [Rogers] tackled difficult issues, like disabilities. He expanded kids' horizons on understanding and aspiration. He raised the bar."[3]

Fred Rogers was born to a wealthy family in Latrobe, Pennsylvania. His childhood was happy in general, but punctuated with difficulties. Fred was introverted, socially isolated, and teased for being overweight. These childhood challenges formed the principles that Mister Rogers lived by, and desired to share with children. His childhood dream was to be a Presbyterian Minister, an occupation that would allow him to share his fundamental belief: "I don't think anyone can grow unless he's loved exactly as he is now, appreciated for what he is rather than what he will be."[4]

Fred Rogers studied music at Rollins College in Winter Park Florida at the time when television was new. He became enthusiastic about the enormous potential of the new medium for reaching people. In 1951, Rogers graduated from college, and took his first job with NBC in New York City. Work in broadcasting resulted in a change from Fred's original career of the Ministry to educational television. His experience in communications resulted in a growing desire to broadcast universal moral and ethical values and lessons to children.

After three years with NBC in New York, Rogers moved to Pittsburgh to create and produce *The Children's Corner*, a successful local television show that used puppets to entertain and educate children. As his career in educational programming was getting started, Fred could not let go of his interest in serving as a spiritual leader.

Torn between continuing his work for children and a career in the ministry, Fred was able to continue both paths at once by enrolling part-time in the Pittsburgh Theological Seminary.[5] This arrangement allowed Rogers to pursue his view of community: "Imagine what our real neighborhoods would be like if each of us offered, as a matter of course, just one kind word to another person."[6]

Rogers completed his graduate degree in theology and maintained his Presbyterian credentials throughout his life. While in seminary, Rogers shared his passion for educational television for children with his teachers, who recommended that he meet with Margaret McFarland, a child development expert at the University of Pittsburgh.

McFarland worked with the pioneers of child development at Pittsburgh's Arsenal Family and Children's Center. The center included Benjamin Spock, the best-selling author of *Baby and Child Care*, renowned development psychologist and Nobel Laureate Erik Erikson, and pediatrician cable television host of "What Every Baby Knows," Dr. T. Berry Brazelton. These leaders believed that parents and other adults should pay more attention to children. Rogers worked closely with McFarland throughout his entire career, using pioneering research in child development as a foundation for his television show.

In 1968, Fred Rogers was invited to create and produce a new show, *Mister Rogers' Neighborhood*, expanding his influence from local viewers to a national audience. The show fused Rogers' three deep interests: children's educational television, the ministry, and child development. The show emphasized children's social and emotional needs, rather than cognitive learning. Rogers carefully crafted episodes that developed children's feelings and ethical reasoning. Mister Rogers approach was to be enthusiastic about healthy things.

EXTRAVAGANT AFFIRMATION

Mister Rogers emphasized affirmation above all other teacher objectives: "The world needs a sense of worth, and it will achieve it only by its people feeling that they are worthwhile."[7] Teachers who embrace the philosophies and pedagogical views of Mister Rogers, which are based on theology and childhood development, will recognize the enormous benefits of affirmation of students and other teachers. Affirmation of students builds a relationship of trust between a teacher and students, enhancing the learning environment. Mister Rogers provided justification for taking the teacher's role seriously.

Teachers are typically busy, and know that they must manage their time effectively to achieve their full potential in the classroom. Mister Rogers highlighted mindful reflection on educational practices and outcomes: "You rarely have time for everything you want in this life, so you need to make choices. And hopefully your choices can come from a deep sense of who you are."[8] For teachers, the desire to improve the lives of others is paramount. Mister Rogers confirms this objective: "Real strength has to do with helping others."[9] Teachers who seek to implement their desire to empower others will find new reserves of energy and satisfaction.

Mister Rogers shared his enormous joy of teaching and helping others learn with child viewers. His blatant love of his work gave him an uncanny confidence in what he is doing that is obvious to viewers. Mister Rogers summarized his own joy by alluding to others: "The thing I remember best about successful people I've met all through the years is their obvious delight in what they're doing and it seems to have very little to do with worldly success. They just love what they're doing, and they love it in front of others."[10]

Rogers' slow and reassuring delivery gave children time to think about what was being said, and to respond. He also provided time for students to respond, called "wait time." Experienced educators know that wait time is a powerful tool for good teaching. They also know the importance of listening carefully and attentively to each student response. Students have important things to share, and effective instructors can usefully imitate Fred Rogers by listening with respect and attention, and providing affirming and thoughtful responses.

Rogers emphasized each day's lesson through repetition. Teachers who follow Rogers' exemplary methods of appropriate pacing, providing a variety of delivery methods, and repetition will create enhanced learning environments, lectures, and videos. Student interest will be intensified, and student learning enriched.

IMPERFECT HERO

To many, Mister Rogers appeared to be perfect in every way. He disagreed: "I'm far from perfect."[11] Mister Rogers struggled with anger, conflict, and self-doubt throughout his career and life. As effective as Mister Rogers was at communicating with children, he often struggled with adult interactions. Many adults found his slow, deliberate manner and unbridled optimism off-putting and insincere.

After twenty productive years of children's education television, Mister Rogers quit his show with the desire to reach an adult audience. For four years, Rogers produced several televised specials, as well as a documentary series, *Old Friends . . . New Friends*. Biographer Maxwell King summarized the experience: "Fred's instinct for talking with children with joy and natural grace just didn't translate to adult television."[12]

One of the themes of *Mister Rogers Neighborhood* is how to deal with mistakes and disappointments. Following his own advice to children, Mister Rogers returned to the activity of his greatest strength: *Mister Rogers' Neighborhood*. He remained there for another two decades.

PATTI SMITH'S PERFORMANCE TO HONOR BOB DYLAN

Patti Smith is a punk rock icon, known for her uncompromising values, artistic approach to songwriting, and strong connection to her audience during performances. Her raw, emotional songs and approachable personality have endeared her to millions of devoted fans over many decades. Smith began her career as a poet, but entered the music industry in 1974, when she "really thought most rock and roll stunk . . . if somebody didn't get in there and start working, it was going to become a big business instead of a powerful force for us kids, myself included."[13] Her sincerity and desire to make the world a better place are apparent in all that Smith does.

Like Fred Rogers, Smith had childhood ambitions to "be something special" in her life, to be a Missionary or a schoolteacher.[14] Smith set out to change rock and roll with her innovative approach of merging poetry with music. Like Mister Rogers and Martin Luther King, Jr. (chapter 11), Smith believes that when you are doing something that you love and believe in, it gives you strength. Smith was inducted into the Rock and Roll Hall of Fame in 2007.

Patti Smith's intellectual approach to entertainment resulted in music that changed the artistic standards of the highly commercialized entertainment industry. Smith exhibits enormous dedication to all of her endeavors, including poetry, art, photography, music, and writing. At the height of her success, Smith took time out from her music career to raise a family.

With two young children at home, she adopted the highly disciplined practice of writing between five and eight o'clock each morning, while her husband and children slept. Her efforts led to the National Book Award for her memoir, *Just Kids*.[15] Like Mister Rogers, Patti Smith's success is characterized by high expectations, uncompromising standards, and enormous ambition to a final product that will inspire the world.

In December 2016, Smith was asked to perform at the Nobel Prize ceremony honoring Bob Dylan's Nobel Prize in Literature. Dylan's prize was controversial: it was the first to be bestowed upon a musician. Previous Nobel Laureates of Literature include William Faulkner, Ernest Hemingway, and Albert Camus (explored in chapter 6). Many traditionalists were opposed to awarding the Nobel Prize to a singer-songwriter. The ceremony took place in Stockholm, attended by the Swedish royal family and Nobel Prize winners from other fields.

Patti Smith had selected one of Dylan's early songs, "A Hard Rain's A-Gonna Fall," a seven-minute ballad based on a question-and-response refrain style of a seventeenth-century folk narrative. Dylan wrote the song in 1962, at age twenty-one. Smith was to perform the song accompanied by an orchestra in place of her rock ensemble. She had loved the song since she was a teenager, and it was one of her late husband's favorite songs.[16]

Once the song was approved by the Nobel ceremony officials, Smith went to work: "From that moment, every spare minute was spent practicing it, making certain that I knew and could convey every line. . . . I sang the words to myself, over and over, in the original key, with pleasure and resolve. I had it in my mind to sing the song exactly as it was written and as well as I was capable of doing."[17]

The audience was elegantly dressed in designer dresses and tuxedos. Awards were bestowed, acceptance speeches delivered, and classical music played by the Royal Stockholm Philharmonic Orchestra. King Carl XVI Gustaf, Queen Silvia, and Crown Princess Victoria were seated on stage in royal attire, directly in front of the performer. Patti Smith, the punk rock legend, respected for her creativity and known for her raucous live concerts, took the stage. Dressed in a navy blazer and white dress shirt, her long gray hair loose, unkempt, with small accent braids on each shoulder. Smith started the song well, but appeared nervous.

During the second verse, Smith froze. She stopped singing, and for several moments looked child-like, fragile, helpless. Those in attendance, and viewers of the performance on the Internet, immediately experienced great empathy, and a desire to flee; to not watch; to turn away from the artist's deep humiliation. Smith recalls, "I was stuck with a plethora of emotions, avalanching with such intensity that I was unable to negotiate them."[18]

Smith apologized to the audience and the orchestra, "I'm sorry . . . I'm sorry . . . I apologize, sorry I'm so nervous."[19] She looked desperately at the royal family, directly in front of her, only feet away. It appeared that the performance would not continue, but the audience's desire to help her succeed was palpable. Everyone in attendance was pulling for the distraught singer. Smith asked the orchestra to "start over." She began to sing again. Confidence rising, Smith's voice was stronger after the disruption; her apology and confession appeared to be purifying, therapeutic, and energizing.

Yet, she struggled a second time, later in the song. Nevertheless, she persisted. The audience's strong yearning for her success provided energy to the struggling artist. Princess Victoria was visibly thrilled with the performance, as were most of the well-dressed attendees. Many of the audience members were moved to tears by the powerful emotional experience, captured musically by the lonely wail of a steel guitar and Dylan's lyrics. The climactic final lines of the ballad were delivered by Smith in Dylanesque fashion: hard hitting, confident, rebellious.

The next morning at breakfast, Smith felt humiliated and ashamed in the presence of the Nobel Laureates. But then, something beautiful happened. The Nobel scientists approached Smith and "showed appreciation for my very public struggle. They told me I did a good job. I wish I would have done better, I said. No, no, they replied, none of us wish that. For us, your performance seemed a metaphor for our own struggles."[20] Several of the 2016 Nobel Prize winners asked to have a selfie taken with Patti Smith as they thanked her for her shaky performance and perseverance.

Mister Rogers addressed this common human experience: "Confronting our feelings and giving them appropriate expression always takes strength, not weakness."[21] Patti Smith is widely known and respected for her thoughtful approach to music, writing, and life, as reflected in her summary of the Nobel performance: "Words of kindness continued through the day, and in the end I had to come to terms with the truer nature of my duty. Why do we commit to our work? Why do we perform? It is above all for the entertainment and transformation of the people. It is all for them."[22]

MISTER ROGERS ON FAILURE

Mister Rogers often shared his mistakes on the air. During one episode's opening song, Mister Rogers missed a button while buttoning his sweater.

Even though this was his trademark opening scene, he laughed and used the error to explain to children that mistakes help us grow and learn: "How great it is when we come to know that times of disappointment can be followed by times of fulfillment."[23]

On another show, Mister Rodgers was singing a song with a group of children, "Head and shoulders, baby / one, two, three / knees and ankles." While the children kept pace with the song, Mister Rogers became completely mixed up: he was touching his head and shoulders while the others were on knees and toes. Not only did Mister Rogers find his mistake funny, but he refused to cut the scene from the show: "we're going to keep it. I want children to know that it's hard to learn something new, and that grownups make mistakes."[24]

Fred Rogers, keenly aware of the experience of failure, shared it with children in his television audience: "Everybody makes mistakes once in a while."[25] All teachers have given a lecture, classroom lesson, or speech that did not go as well as planned. These failed presentations are painful, especially if they are recorded. Mister Rogers offers a way forward. His approach was to use mistakes to learn and grow, emphasizing that what really matters is how you react to making a mistake. "Often out of periods of losing come the greatest strivings toward a new winning streak."[26]

Patti Smith endorsed this course of action in her commencement speech to Pratt Institute graduates: "You know who you are, even when sometimes it becomes a little blurry and you make mistakes or seem to be veering off, just go deeper. You know who you are. You know the right thing to do. And when you make a mistake, it's alright—just as the song goes, pick yourself up, brush yourself off, and start all over again."[27]

Teachers know this; teachers teach this. However, this knowledge can be difficult to recall when errors occur. Not only do instructors obsess over what went wrong, but it is easy to become immobilized by mistakes. The simple truth of Fred Rogers can help move educators forward: "Often when you think you're at the end of something, you're at the beginning of something else."[28]

CONCLUSION

Fred Rogers summarized his philosophy on making mistakes: "It may be that the most important mastery we achieve early on is not the mastery of a particular skill or particular piece of knowledge, but rather the mastery of the patience and persistence that learning requires, along with the ability to expect and accept mistakes and the feelings of disappointment they may bring."[29]

Not only was Mister Rogers unafraid of mistakes, he embraced errors. His philosophy of teaching included acceptance of mistakes made by teachers and others in authority positions. This can be a powerful tool if used in the classroom. Instructors who encourage students to point out mistakes in lectures, course materials, and assessments will be rewarded with engaged students excitedly seeking to find problems, contradictions, or typographical errors in the course.

Confident teachers can encourage feedback, and praise students who provide corrections or constructive comments. This application of Mister Rogers' teachings can be formalized by offering students extra credit for pointing out errors. Students who point out an error could earn a positive reward from the instructor, making them proud, and ready to identify the next error. When teachers effectively encourage and reward feedback, trust between students and their teacher is amplified. Mister Rogers viewed mistakes as productive tools: classroom mistakes can lead to good outcomes!

INTERSECTIONS

In 1969, Mister Rogers invited a black officer to join him in a pool, during a time when racial tensions were high, and pools still segregated. He displayed on television, to his huge audience of children (the next generation), that diversity is good. Thank you, #MisterRogers.

—Martin Luther King III, (@officialMLK3, July 24, 2019).[30]

If biographers are ethically bound to provide as well-rounded a portrait of their subjects as possible, what happens when they profile people who are virtually flawless? Saintly figures like Mother Teresa, Gandhi, Jesus make the job of biography challenging—and so, it turns out, does Fred Rogers.

—Tina Hassannia[31]

TEACHING SUMMARY: TEACH WITH KINDNESS LIKE MISTER ROGERS

- Be kind.
- Be honest and sincere.
- Carefully plan and review for class, including delivery, message, content, attitude, impact, and meaning.
- Each lesson or lecture should be well-planned and intentional, but it will not be perfect. Mistakes will happen, and students will learn from the imperfections.

- Proactively consider how your lessons will impact student learning, student emotions, and the desire to learn.
- Use delivery pace, variety, and repetition to maximize student attention and learning.
- Recognize that mistakes, obstacles, and failure are a common feature of all teachers and teaching. All teachers, Nobel Prize winners, and rock stars experience the sting of failure.
- Recall the importance of teachers and teaching.

NOTES

1. Rogers, *World According*, 124.
2. Rogers, *Life's Journeys*, 95.
3. King, *Good Neighbor*, 7.
4. McDowell, "Most Inspiring."
5. King, *Good Neighbor*, 113.
6. Rogers, *World According*, 159.
7. Rogers, *World According*, 149.
8. Rogers, *World According*, 30.
9. Rogers, *World According*, 39.
10. Rogers, *World According*, 40.
11. Dailymotion, "Rogers' Neighborhood."
12. King, *Good Neighbor*, 240.
13. Young, "People Too."
14. Young, "People Too."
15. Smith, *Just Kids*.
16. Smith, "How Does?"
17. Smith, "How Does?"
18. Smith, "How Does?"
19. Nobel Prize Award Ceremony, "2016 Nobel."
20. Smith, "How Does?"
21. Rogers, *World According*, 14.
22. Smith, "How Does?"
23. Rogers, *World According*, 91.
24. King, *Good Neighbor*, 9.
25. Dailymotion, "Rogers' Neighborhood."
26. Rogers, *World According*, 101.
27. Smith, "Commencement Address."
28. Rogers, *World According*, 38.
29. Rogers, *Life's Journeys*, 123.
30. King, Martin Luther III. "Rogers Tweet."
31. Hassannia, "Never Known."

REFERENCES

Dailymotion. "Mister Rogers' Neighborhood Episode 15x80." Accessed February 8, 2021. https://www.dailymotion.com/video/x3t5sqq

Hassannia, Tina. "The World has Never Known How to Respond to Someone as Positive as Mr. Rogers." *National Post*, June 7, 2018. https://nationalpost.com/entertainment/movies/the-world-has-never-known-how-to-respond-to-someone-as-positive-as-mr-rogers

King, Martin Luther III. "Mister Rogers Tweet." *Twitter*, July 24, 2019. Accessed February 10, 2021. https://twitter.com/officialmlk3/status/1154176898139938816?lang=en

King, Maxwell. *The Good Neighbor: The Life and Work of Fred Rogers*. New York: Abrams, 2018.

McDowell, Erin. "12 of the Most Inspiring Fred Rogers Quotes to Get You through Any Crisis." *Business Insider*, March 24, 2020. https://www.businessinsider.com/inspiring-mr-rogers-quotes-about-helping-others

Nobel Prize Award Ceremony. Stockholm, Sweden Concert Hall. December 10, 2016. The Nobel Prize in Literature 2016. Accessed January 21, 2021. https://www.nobelprize.org/prizes/literature/2016/award-video/

Rogers, Fred. *Life's Journeys According to Mister Rogers: Things to Remember Along the Way*. New York: Hachette Books; Revised edition, 2019.

Rogers, Fred. *The World According to Mister Rogers: Important Things to Remember*. New York: Hachette Books; Revised edition, 2019.

Smith, Patti. "How Does It Feel?" *The New Yorker*, December 14, 2016. Accessed January 21, 2021. https://www.newyorker.com/culture/cultural-comment/patti-smith-on-singing-at-bob-dylans-nobel-prize-ceremony

Smith, Patti. *Just Kids*. New York: HarperCollins, 2010.

Smith, Patti. Pratt Institute Commencement Address. Brooklyn, New York, May 2010. Accessed February 8, 2021. https://www.brainpickings.org/2014/04/21/patti-smith-pratt-commencement/

Young, Michael. "Kids are People Too." Patti Smith interview conducted by Michael Young in 1979. Accessed February 8, 2021. https://www.youtube.com/watch?v=Agl4IvNnQPo

Chapter 4

Purpose from Doubt

Mother Teresa

Figure 4.1   Mother Teresa. *Source*: Wikimedia Commons. Turelio. Creative Commons CC-BY-SA-2.0 de.

Be faithful in small things because it is in them that your strength lies.
—Mother Teresa[1]

*All saw her courageous struggle in establishing her work, her outgoing
love for the poor and suffering, the care for her Sisters; but the spiritual
darkness remained her secret. She seemed cheerful in her daily life,
tireless in her work. The inner agony would not weaken her activities.*
—Jesuit Father Joseph Neuner, Mother
Teresa's correspondent and confidante[2]

CHAPTER SYNOPSIS

Mother Teresa's notable work with people who are poor motivates teachers
to give their best effort to all students, without exception. Teresa's call to
service provides an inspiration to educators who feel that teaching is meaningful, and the best possible job for them. Teachers can emulate Teresa by
identifying and pursuing the activity with the greatest room for improvement
of student learning outcomes. Teresa suffered deep personal doubts about her
own religion and spirituality, yet continued her inspiring work throughout her
life. Knowledge of Teresa's lifetime struggle with "the darkness" can help
teachers move forward in times of difficulty.

Do you believe that you were somehow meant to be a teacher? Have you met
a teacher who claims that he or she was called to be a teacher? Many educators' identity and sense of purpose are based on the feeling that they love
being a teacher, and that they are in a highly meaningful profession. Teachers
who claim to have such a *calling* show more *commitment* to the idea of a
teaching career and are less concerned about the *sacrifices* required by the
teaching profession.[3] The life of Mother Teresa can be summarized by these
three principles: a calling, commitment, and sacrifice.

Teresa was born in 1910, called to be a nun in 1928, and called a second
time in 1946 to serve "the poorest of the poor." In 1950, she founded the
Missionaries of Charity in Calcutta (now Kolkata) India. Teresa's well-
known charity provides food, clothing, shelter, and comfort to destitute, out-
cast, sick, and dying people throughout the world: people who are suffering.
Teresa's lifelong commitment to helping the poor led to the rapid growth and
global reach of the Missionaries of Charity. Her unique contribution resulted
in canonization of Teresa as a Saint by the Catholic Church in 2016 for her
dedicated service to the world's most needy people.

Teresa was subject to massive, unrelenting self-doubt and spiritual darkness for most of her life, made public in 2007, years after her death in 1997.[4]

Teresa's extraordinary life of giving to the poor can inspire teachers to enhance their service to others, and carry educators through difficulties, both professional and personal.

Teresa was born Agnes Bojanxhiu in Skopje, North Macedonia, to prosperous parents. At age eighteen, Agnes left her loving family to join the Sisters of Loreto, a Roman Catholic religious congregation of women dedicated to education in Rathfarnham, Ireland. As an enthusiastic missionary, she sacrificed life with her family to provide assistance to others.

Upon joining the Order, Agnes adopted the name Sister Teresa. Within a year, Teresa moved to Darjeeling, India. In 1931, she took religious vows of poverty, chastity, and obedience, as well as a promise to devote herself to the instruction of youth. Teresa was appointed to a teaching position at St. Mary's Bengali Medium School for girls in Calcutta. In 1937, she took her final vows, and became Mother Teresa, a title customarily given to Loreto nuns.

Teresa worked excessively hard as a teacher, causing her to become ill from exhaustion in 1946. Her doctors recommended a retreat, intended as a physical break from work, and an opportunity for spiritual renewal. During the break from work, Teresa felt a strong calling to redirect her life from teaching to aiding "the poorest of the poor." After a period of learning and development, she founded the Sisters of Charity in 1950, committed to helping the poorest people of Calcutta, among the poorest cities in the world.

Teresa's life was one of sacrifice. She shared that "To leave Loreto was my greatest sacrifice, the most difficult thing I have ever done. It was much more difficult than to leave my family and country. In Loreto I have received my spiritual training."[5] Teresa's move from the safety and protection of the convent to the danger of the slums required courage and sacrifice. She did not know how drastically the new work would change her inner life and faith.

Teresa established the unique mission of her new charity: "to carry Christ into the homes and streets of the slums, among the sick, dying, the beggars and the little street children. The sick will be nursed as far as possible in their poor homes. The little children will have a school in the slums. The beggars will be sought and visited in their holes outside the town or on the streets."[6] The mission statement was later extended to include the poorest of the poor all over the globe.

How did Teresa help the poor? Through simplicity in action: "Not all of us can do great things. But we can do small things with great love."[7] Mother Teresa described her contribution: "I believe in person-to-person contact . . . the person I am meeting is the one person in the world at that moment."[8] When meeting people, Teresa's advice is of supreme importance: "Kind words can be short and easy to speak, but their echoes are truly endless."[9] Teachers have deep knowledge and experience with this truth.

Father Brian Kolodiejchuk, M.C., Director of the Mother Teresa Center, concluded, "People of all creeds and walks of life recognized her selfless love and compassion for the poor; they admired her simplicity and genuineness and were attracted by the joy and peace that radiated from her."[10] Not all teachers can be as compassionate as Mother Teresa. However, all teachers can move toward her level of effectiveness. Teresa did not become a saint overnight, she moved continuously toward her goals over a long period of time.

Teresa was awarded the Nobel Peace Prize in 1979 "for work undertaken in the struggle to overcome poverty and distress, which also constitutes a threat to peace."[11] She also earned the US Medal of Freedom, and the United Nations Albert Schweitzer Prize for Humanitarianism. Teresa continued to live simply and provide service to others throughout her life, until her death in 1997. The Missionaries of Charity grew to approximately 450 brothers and 5,000 sisters worldwide, operating 600 missions, schools, and shelters in 120 countries.[12]

A CALL TO TEACH

Chilean professor of education policy Cristobal Madero reports that "The concept of calling pervades the world of teachers and education."[13] A professional "calling" is often a religious, spiritual, or transcendental experience. Divine intervention is one important way to receive a call to teach. Alternatively, education professor and psychology scholar Clifford Mayes suggests that a teaching career can be interpreted from a mythical point of view as a "Hero's Journey." The hero's myth begins with a call, announced in a dream, delivered by a mystical animal, or issued as a challenge from an authority figure.[14]

For Mayes, the Hero's Journey is a symbol of emotional, intellectual, and spiritual growth that an individual experiences as "he or she goes beyond the narrow confines of family and immediate environment in order to seek, find, and ultimately act on a new vision of self, society, world, and cosmos."[15] Teresa's life followed a similar path.

Some teachers may experience a religious calling or a hero's calling to teach. These types of call, however, are not the only way that teachers can feel called. Education writer and scholar Parker Palmer suggests that "any authentic call ultimately comes from the voice of the teacher within, the voice that invites me to honor the nature of my true self."[16] Those who are "called to teach" are teachers who feel that they are doing what they were meant to do; or teachers who believe that they are in the best of all possible occupations.

Defined this way, the call to teach emphasizes a willingness and desire to serve students, to promote learning and the improvement of others. The acceptance of a teacher's role, responsibility, and commitment is perhaps the main characteristic of the journey to become a teacher. For some, this occurs at a specific time and place as a "call to teach." For others, it may be a process, and evolve over time.

David Hansen, an expert in the philosophy of teaching, writes: "The passion of dedicated teachers encompasses their deepest aspirations to achieve a meaningful life for students and themselves. Teachers find intense fulfillment in contributing to students' well-being, or in a breakthrough with a struggling colleague, or in a rewarding communication with a parent or guardian."[17] Teachers who share these experiences are considered to have a "call to teach."

Bradley Conrad, an experienced teacher, writer, department chair, teacher educator, and student teacher advisor identifies five qualities of those who have been called to teach: (1) care, (2) a desire to serve, (3) open-mindedness, (4) resiliency, and (5) a desire to make the world a better place.[18] Of these, Conrad identifies care as the most important: "For many caring is the essence of teaching . . . the best teachers possess an attitude of service, when they receive great satisfaction and even joy from serving others."[19]

Teachers can learn a great deal from the life trajectory of Saint Teresa, noting that her calling evolved over the course of her life. Teresa's progression from a religious child to a teacher to a provider of assistance to the poor demonstrates how occupational development can require time, reflection, and openness to change. Teresa was a committed teacher for nearly twenty years before experiencing her second call to her ultimate occupation. Careers in teaching also evolve over time toward a teacher's true self, often toward a deeper commitment of service.

COMMITMENT

Mother Teresa lived a productive and effective life, with simplicity as a guidepost. Her commitment to the poorest of the poor is an inspirational call to service for all people, but also provides a specific lesson for teachers. Many educators ask, what is the best way to spend my time? Economics, together with Teresa's life, provide direction.

Economics is the study of how to choose between options. Choices are necessary in a world where our wants, needs, and desires outweigh our ability to pay for them. The human condition is defined by scarcity: the sad condition that we can't have everything that we want. We are forced to choose between competing options: a new car or new clothes; a vacation or restaurant meal; time spent at work or with family?

Under such circumstances, our choices define who we are, and determine our impact on others. The fundamental principle of economics is to allocate resources to the activity with the highest return. This principle is often applied to financial investments and economic decisions, but it can also provide insight and guidance to personal and professional choices. In particular, this rule for greater efficiency can be applied to teaching decisions, course improvement, and interpersonal success.

The fundamental questions of "how should I spend my time," "what could I do to improve my course," and "how could I improve student learning outcomes" can all be usefully addressed with the economic way of thinking and by Teresa's life story. Teresa devoted her life to what was for her the activity with the largest impact on the world: a calling to help the poor. Likewise, teachers can devote their thought, time, and energy to the highest impact activity.

At times, important activities can be ignored or overlooked, because they can be the least favorite things for a teacher to do. For example, some educators enjoy the rewards that come from student interaction, providing encouragement, and sharing knowledge with others. These teachers may be less interested in writing course assignments, lesson plans, or lectures. The economic principle suggests giving greater attention to the weakest part of the class, as that is where the greatest gains can be made.

Other teachers may have great disciplinary knowledge, and be experts on course content. This group may be less interested or capable at student interactions and relationships. Devoting more time to working with people can often deliver large gains in teacher confidence, student experience, and learning outcomes. Greater student engagement can lead to better student learning outcomes and higher achievement.

Human nature can cause teachers to avoid the activity with the highest returns, whether it be course material, delivery method, positive interactions, grading and returning assignments in a timely fashion, or any number of teaching tasks, strategies, or activities. Many people across the globe ignored the poorest of the poor until Teresa prioritized the issue and widely and effectively communicated the need for such work.

Recall that Teresa's vows included poverty, chastity, and obedience. In the early development of Teresa's organization, the Missionaries of Charity, she was known for asking, begging, and pleading with nearby merchants for food, clothing, and money. This seems to contradict her vow of poverty, but these resources were used only to provide for people who needed them. Rather than only using the meager resources of a nun, Teresa continued to boldly raise funds throughout her life. Teresa was again allocating her effort to the activity of highest returns: gathering financial resources for the improvement of the poorest of the poor.

SACRIFICE

In 2007, it was revealed that Teresa had spent most of her life in "terrible darkness." In a letter to her spiritual director and confidante Father Neuner, Teresa described her spiritual life: "this terrible sense of loss—this untold darkness—this loneliness—this continual longing for God—which give me that pain deep down in my heart. —Darkness is such that I really do not see— . . . there is no God in me. . . . He is not there. . . . God does not want me."[20]

Teresa's agonizing account of her deep spiritual life and daily practices expresses her persistent and unyielding pain. Teresa did not allow her own spiritual suffering to hinder her work. Father Brian Kolodiejchuk writes, "Although this intense and ongoing spiritual agony could have made her despondent, she instead radiated remarkable joy and love."[21]

Many spiritual practices and traditions consider the type of suffering experienced by Teresa as a "dark night of the soul," referring to painful purifications that are experienced before reaching harmony with a higher power. Mother Teresa shows the way forward for teachers in times of turmoil, self-doubt, and difficulty by facing her deep pain with no reduction in her desire to help others. Teachers who practice "self-care" by managing their own mental health and emotional needs can bring more energy to serving others, and thus have a greater positive impact on the world.

Teresa's resiliency matches teacher and instructional coach Bradley Conrad's view of teaching: "Teaching is hard. It's incredibly rewarding but hard . . . we have to not only be willing to never give up on a child, but we have to continue to come back, day after day, and try to reach even the most resistant of students."[22] Not only is teaching challenging, but Conrad continues: "We are going to fail. We are not always going to reach every kid, no matter how hard we try, but we have to persist in trying."[23]

Remaining open to the changing needs of others allows teachers to have great impact in small ways. Conrad explains the characteristics of open-mindedness: "I have found that a good teacher educator can help any person develop into a good teacher so long as they possess an open-minded orientation. Open-minded teachers are self-reflective, open to feedback, and willing to change and try new things."[24]

A flexible mindset toward change and improvement allows for continuous personal and professional growth for successful teachers. Open-minded teachers are willing to "assess norms, customs, or rules and to challenge those aspects where they believe it to be appropriate."[25] Conrad's view of teachers mirrors the life of Mother Teresa: "Teaching is about giving. . . . I have never met a good teacher who got into this profession that in some way didn't do it so as to make the world a better place. The impact we have on the lives our students are innumerable and immeasurable."[26]

For five decades, Teresa felt no presence of God, either in her work or in her spiritual life, beginning at the time of her second call in 1946, until her death in 1997. The only exception was a five-week period in 1959. In her letters to her spiritual directors, Teresa described her pain as undergoing "dryness," "darkness," "loneliness," and "torture."[27] She compared the darkness with hell, and at one point, she doubted the existence of heaven and God. With the exception of her spiritual advisors, no one knew this during Teresa's life, not even her Sisters in the Missionaries of Charity.

Far from hypocrisy or anti-religious views, Teresa's absence of God is considered by many spiritual traditions as a common occurrence in a faithful life. In fact, Kolodiejchuk sees her darkness as evidence of perseverance and "her most spiritual heroic act."[28] Dr. Richard Gottlieb, a teacher and psychoanalyst, explains: "What is remarkable is that she integrated it in a way that enable her to make it the organizing center of her personality, the beacon for her ongoing spiritual life."[29]

Religious writer David Van Biema suggests that the most important implication of Teresa's suffering and darkness is "that if she could carry on for a half-century without God in her head or heart, then perhaps people not quite as saintly can cope with less extreme versions of the same problem."[30]

Teresa's powerful faith in the face of silence shows that even the most effective, holy, and kind people suffer from self-doubt. Many educators suffer from insecurity about their profession, classes, students, and colleagues. Teresa provides the realization that this is common. Moreover, she shows that the most successful people may be the ones who suffer the most. Her example is one of maintaining effort and commitment in times of trouble. This is the teacher's calling: stick with it, you are not alone, do good anyway.

CONCLUSION

Mother Teresa dedicated her life to improving the lives of those with the greatest needs. Her life and actions are remarkably similar to what Gandhi shared as his method for eliminating self-doubt (chapter 9). A talisman is an object with religious or magical powers intended to protect the individual who carries it, or a good luck charm. In 1947, Gandhi wrote a note that began: "I will give you a talisman. Whenever you are in doubt, or when the self becomes too much with you, apply the following test."[31]

Gandhi continued, "Recall the face of the poorest and the weakest man (or woman) whom you may have seen, and ask yourself, if the step you contemplate is going to be of any use to him (her). Will it restore him (her) to a control over his (her) own life and destiny? Then you will find your doubts and yourself melt away."[32] Mother Teresa's life is the epitome of this talisman.

Angela Watson, an experienced teacher and instructional coach, emphasizes that self-doubt is a natural part of being reflective and wanting to be your very best: "Anyone who is analyzing their work and striving to be better is going to feel like an imposter at times."[33] Follow the path of Mother Teresa by using your doubt and insecurity to become better.

Reflection on teaching practices and identification of the teaching activity with the greatest impact will allow teachers to make progress and improve. In the process, self-doubt will be reduced or eliminated. Teresa shows us the power of personal struggle: accept your situation but even more than that, use doubt and suffering to prosper. Service to others is a teacher's *call* to teach, the *commitment* to making the world a better place, and the *sacrifice* for the common good. Teresa challenges all teachers: "Yesterday is gone. Tomorrow has not yet come. We have only today. Let us begin."[34]

INTERSECTIONS

A loss to the entire humanity. She will be deeply missed in our efforts to build international peace, and a just, caring and equitable world order.

—South African president Nelson Mandela[35]

Mahatma Gandhi and Mother Teresa are India's pride and envy of the world. They were the ultimate symbols of harmony, humanism and compassion in a world driven by conflict, politics, religion, gender, greed, money power and much else.

—Dominic Thomas[36]

TEACHING SUMMARY: PREVAIL OVER DARKNESS LIKE MOTHER TERESA

- Think of the teaching profession as a call; or doing what you were meant to do. Internalize the idea that teaching is the best possible job for you.
- Follow Teresa by adopting the call to serve others, and promote student learning.
- Consider teacher development as a lifelong process. Teaching careers often evolve and progress toward a teacher's true self and deeper commitment to the service of others.
- Identify the teaching activity of greatest impact, and doggedly pursue it. Choose the activity with the greatest room for improvement, rather than the easiest activity, or the one that is the most comfortable.

- Teaching is difficult. Like Teresa, teachers will experience difficulties and failure. Move forward with the knowledge that Teresa suffered greatly in her darkness, but persevered by enhancing her service to others.
- Teresa shows us the power of personal struggle: accept your situation, and use self-doubt and suffering to prosper.
- Like Teresa, service to others is the teacher's call to teach, commit, and sacrifice.

NOTES

1. Teresa and Kelly, *Something Beautiful*, 16.
2. Teresa, *My Light*, 9.
3. Bullough and Hall-Kenyon, "The Call."
4. Teresa, *My Light*.
5. Teresa and Kelly, *Something Beautiful*, 64.
6. Teresa, *My Light*, 43.
7. Teresa and Kelly, *Something Beautiful*, 116.
8. Teresa and Kelly, *Something Beautiful*, 7.
9. Teresa and Kelly, *Something Beautiful*, 13.
10. Teresa, *My Light*, Preface, ix.
11. Nobel Peace Prize, "Press Release."
12. Slavicek, *Mother Teresa*.
13. Madero, "Because," 1.
14. Mayes, *Hero's Journey*, 12.
15. Mayes, *Hero's Journey*, 11.
16. Palmer, *Courage*, 29.
17. Hansen, "The Call."
18. Conrad, "The Calling."
19. Conrad, "The Calling."
20. Teresa, *My Light*, 2.
21. Teresa, *My Light*, 4
22. Conrad, "The Calling."
23. Conrad, "The Calling."
24. Conrad, "The Calling."
25. McConnell, Conrad, and Uhrmacher, *Lesson Planning*.
26. Conrad, "The Calling."
27. Van Biema, "Crisis of Faith."
28. Van Biema, "Crisis of Faith."
29. Van Biema, "Crisis of Faith."
30. Van Biema, "Crisis of Faith."
31. Thomas, "The Track."
32. Thomas, "The Track."
33. Watson, "Imposter Syndrome."

34. Teresa and Kelly, *Something Beautiful*, 123.
35. Teresa and Kelly, *Something Beautiful*, 2.
36. Thomas, "The Track."

REFERENCES

Bullough, Robert V., and Kendra M. Hall-Kenyon. "The Call to Teach and Teacher Hopefulness." *Teacher Development* 15, no. 2 (May 2011): 127–140. doi: 10.1080/13664530.2011.571488

Conrad, Bradley. "The Calling to Teach." *Tales from Classroom Education Blog*, March 5, 2020. Accessed April 14, 2021. https://talesfromthecla.medium.com/the -calling-to-teach-185ecefa3e04

Hansen, David T. *The Call to Teach*. New York: Teachers College Press, 1995.

Madero, Cristóbal. "Because I Am Called: How a Calling to Teach Emerges and Develops in Teachers Working in Catholic High Schools." *Teaching and Teacher Education* 101 (May 2021): 103319. doi: 10.1016/j.tate.2021.103319.

Mayes, Clifford. *The Archetypal Hero's Journey in Teaching and Learning*. Madison, WI: Atwood Publishing, 2010.

McConnell, Christy, Bradley Conrad, and P. Bruce Uhrmacher. *Lesson Planning with Purpose: Five Approaches to Curriculum Design*. New York: Teachers College Press, 2020.

Nobel Peace Prize 1979. "Press Release." NobelPrize.org. Nobel Media AB 2021. Accessed April 14, 2021. https://www.nobelprize.org/prizes/peace/1979/press -release/

Palmer, Parker J. *The Courage to Teach: Exploring the Inner Landscape of a Teacher's Life*. John Wiley & Sons, 2017.

Slavicek, Louise. *Mother Teresa*. New York: Infobase Publishing, 2007, pp. 90–91.

Teresa, Mother. *Come Be My Light: The Private Writings of the Saint of Calcutta*, ed. Brian Kolodiejchuk. New York: Doubleday, 2007, pp. 185–212.

Teresa, Mother, and Matthew Kelly. *Do Something Beautiful for God: The Essential Teachings of Mother Teresa*. North Palm Beach, FL: Blue Sparrow Books, 2019.

Thomas, Dominic. "The Track to Enlightenment: Mahatma Gandhi and Mother Teresa: The Greatest Indians of the 20th century Found their Calling on Train Journeys." *Union of Catholic Asian News*. October 2, 2020. https://www.ucanews .com/news/the-track-to-enlightenment-mahatma-gandhi-and-mother-teresa/89527

Van Biema, David. "Mother Teresa's Crisis of Faith." *Time Magazine*, August 23, 2007. https://time.com/4126238/mother-teresas-crisis-of-faith/

Watson, Angela. "7 Ways Teachers Can Push Past Imposter Syndrome." *The Cornerstone for Teachers Blog*, November 12, 2017. Accessed April 14, 2021. https://thecornerstoneforteachers.com/truth-for-teachers-podcast/imposter -syndrome/

Chapter 5

Anger and Forgiveness

Malcolm X

Figure 5.1 **Malcolm X.** *Source*: Wikimedia Commons.United States Library of Congress's Prints and Photographs division, digital ID ppmsc.01274.

You have to wake the people up first, then you'll get action.

—Malcolm X[1]

I want to be remembered as someone who was sincere. Even if I made mistakes, they were made in sincerity. If I was wrong, I was wrong in sincerity.

—Malcolm X[2]

CHAPTER SYNOPSIS

Malcolm X's life provides powerful witness to how injustice and oppression can create anger, and how immense anger can be transformed into forgiveness. This chapter highlights how teachers can enhance their ability to help others by adopting Malcolm's strong commitment to the truth, and his dedication to not give up on others, no matter what their background or actions. The National Memorial for Peace and Justice is highlighted to motivate exploration of the causes and consequences of systemic racism, and what teachers could do to move their students and consequently our world toward greater justice in the future.

Readers are drawn to *The Autobiography of Malcom X.*[3] This is the favorite book of many, due to the enormous intensity of the author and his insightful life experience. Filmmaker Spike Lee is one of those readers: "The most important book I'll ever read, it changed the way I thought, it changed the way I acted. It has given me courage I didn't know I had inside me. I'm one of hundreds of thousands whose lives were changed for the better."[4] *The Autobiography of Malcom X* is highly ranked on numerous lists as one of the greatest books.[5]

Malcolm X spoke truth. He spoke truth to power. He also spoke truth to the powerless. Malcolm X's observations and convictions about black rights and life in the United States have remained timely and relevant for over six decades. Malcolm X continues to have an impact on societal views, events, and policies. Teachers who study Malcolm X can benefit enormously from his message, his conviction, and his blunt honesty.

Malcolm X was born in 1925 as Malcolm Little in Omaha, Nebraska to the Reverend Earl Little, an outspoken Baptist Minister, and Louise Little, an activist and branch reporter for the Universal Negro Improvement Association. As a child, Malcolm experienced violent racism stemming from his father's outspoken personality and support of separatist Black Nationalist views of racial segregation.[6] At age four, Malcolm's family home was burned to the ground.

At age six, Malcolm's father was brutally murdered with reports of white racists responsible for his death. His mother tried to keep the family together, but suffered from mental health issues. Malcolm was taken from his mother and placed in foster homes. His mother was institutionalized for twenty-six years. Malcolm cared for her deeply, but rarely saw her during that time.

The story resonates at a deep level. The violence and oppression based on racism and hatred is impossible to turn away from. Malcolm's story seems too extreme to be true; yet, we know that it is the truth. A truth that is new and potent for many readers. In US grade schools, students typically learn about slavery, racism, Martin Luther King, Jr., and the Civil Rights movement. Students may not learn of the brutal reality of living life as a person of color in America. Malcolm's blunt honesty brings this crucial message home.

Malcolm dropped out of school in eighth grade, moved from the Midwest to Boston, and became a street hustler: crime, alcohol, drugs, and guiding potential customers to brothels. His criminal behavior led to his 1946 arrest and conviction for burglary. Malcolm was sentenced to ten years in prison. While incarcerated, Malcolm's life was transformed. During his first year of prison, the other men in his cellblock called him, "Satan" for his enormous anger, antireligious ranting, and vicious cursing attacks.[7]

Later, Malcolm decided to continue his education through correspondence courses after meeting Bimbi, a highly intelligent, well-read, and articulate fellow inmate. Soon, Malcolm had read every book available in the prison library. He abstained from alcohol and drugs, and began to pray. He later explained, "I have often reflected upon the new vistas that reading opened to me. I knew right there in prison that reading had changed forever the course of my life. As I see it today, the ability to read awoke inside me some long dormant craving to be mentally alive."[8]

Malcolm respected some of the other black prisoners, who were members of the Nation of Islam (NOI). The NOI is a religious organization that promotes black empowerment, racial segregation, and Black Nationalism. Malcolm was drawn to the NOI, since these racial views provided a vigorous explanation and response to his childhood and young adult experiences with racism and white oppression. Due to good behavior, Malcolm was paroled after seven years.

Upon release, Malcolm converted to Islam, and replaced the slave name "Little" with "X," to represent his lost African tribal name. Malcolm became a Minister for the NOI, and based on his charisma, keen insight, and powerful speaking ability, quickly rose to the highest levels within the organization. Malcolm's fierce arguments and unyielding convictions resonated with many African Americans, resulting in large numbers of new converts to the NOI, including Muhammad Ali (chapter 1).

Malcolm became a national spokesman for the NOI, and a fervent follower of the group's leader, Elijah Muhammad. During this time, Malcolm developed strong beliefs about black unity, which held the objective of the spiritual, social, political, and economic separation of races. Malcolm promoted black dignity, an idea that has encouraged self-confidence and pride within the African American community, both during and after his life.

Malcolm's militant truth-telling and growing fame led to trouble with both his mentor Elijah Muhammad and the US government. The NOI is not recognized as part of the official mainstream Islam faith, but instead promotes a unique, race-based version of Islam that considers white people "blue-eyed devils" who should be avoided. Malcolm not only subscribed to these beliefs, but zealously promoted them with great success. Malcolm's rhetoric of anger intensified: "Concerning nonviolence, it is criminal to teach a man not to defend himself when he is the constant victim of brutal attacks."[9]

Malcolm's candor was, and remains, exceptional. His willingness to fight for justice with a direct, unforgiving approach drew attention and fear for many individuals, both blacks and whites. Malcolm raged: "If you're not ready to die for it, put the word 'freedom' out of your vocabulary."[10] As Malcolm became more popular, the NOI grew from 500 members in 1952 to 30,000 members in 1963.[11] This enormous success caused alarm and panic for many. The Federal Bureau of Investigation (FBI) began to use bugs, wiretaps, and hidden cameras to surveil Malcolm X. The FBI also infiltrated the NOI.

Devoted to Elijah Muhammad, Malcolm considered him a living prophet and personal savior. Malcolm had obeyed the NOI's strict behavioral rules including abstention from alcohol and drugs, as well as celibacy outside of marriage. He was devastated to later learn of Elijah Muhammad's extramarital affairs with many young NOI women, resulting in several children. Malcolm refused to cover up the affairs of his savior and struggled with the knowledge that he had recruited thousands of new people to a dishonest and deceptive organization, resulting in his departure from the NOI in March 1964.

Malcolm founded a new competing religious organization, the Muslim Mosque Inc. and converted to Sunni Islam, the largest mainstream branch of Islam. Malcolm switched to Sunni beliefs that promote universal racial brotherhood, a major divergence from his prior racist, segregationist beliefs of the NOI. Malcolm X participated in Hajj, the pilgrimage to Mecca. This journey changed his life and worldview. He spent time with and enjoyed pilgrims of all races.

Upon his return to the United States, Malcolm no longer considered white people to be "blue-eyed devils," but instead said that he had met "blonde-haired, blued-eyed men I could call my brothers."[12] Malcolm adopted an important message for all races, and now considered racial integration a hope for the future: "I'm for truth, no matter who tells it. I'm for justice, no matter who it's for or against."[13] This was a stunning transformation for Malcolm, coincident with his name change from Malcolm X to El-Hajj Malik El-Shabazz.

Upon return to the United States from Mecca, Malcolm faced numerous, continued threats from the NOI throughout 1964. His assessment was characteristically blunt: "It is a time for martyrs now, and if I am to be one, it will be for the cause of brotherhood. That's the only thing that can save this country."[14] Two days after making this statement, on February 21, 1965, Malcolm X was murdered at age thirty-nine by NOI followers loyal to Elijah Muhammad.

SHARING REDEMPTION WITH OTHERS

Malcolm X promoted the idea of self-reinvention for self-improvement: "There is no better than adversity. Every defeat, every heartbreak, every loss, contains its own seed, its own lesson on how to improve your performance the next time."[15] An example illustrates this important point. During the Coronavirus pandemic, most classrooms and courses necessarily changed formats mid-semester from live lectures to online. After the rapid move to online learning, many instructors held live Internet sessions to replace live, face-to-face lectures.

At first, some teachers hurried through the course material in a perfunctory manner, in the attempt to not waste students' time. The move to the online framework was stressful. Simple, mechanical presentations were in many cases an effort to keep the courses moving forward without interruption or complication. Later, many teachers revised their formats by incorporating current events into their lessons.

A candid discussion of complicated and contentious topics related to the pandemic could include face masks, food safety, social distancing, public gatherings, closing schools, vaccines, and the impact of the pandemic on the food supply. Examples can produce a huge improvement in student learning. Teachers shared a deeper truth with students, and students enthusiastically appreciated the change. Participation in online sessions that incorporate current events is more lively, interesting, and contentious. This simple pedagogical change can be hugely successful.

At the height of the pandemic, the brutal murder of African American George Floyd was recorded in Minneapolis. The Black Lives Matter movement and months of daily protest provided an opportunity to bring crucial events to classrooms. When teachers share their experiences, attitudes, and beliefs about current events, students benefit from honesty and sincerity. Some will be critical of this type of pedagogy. Malcolm X knew this well: "If you have no critics, you'll likely have no success."[16]

TEACHING AND FORGIVENESS

After years of promoting and defending separatism, segregation, and violence, Malcolm X discovered awareness, enlightenment, and ultimately, forgiveness. This is perhaps Malcolm's greatest gift: teachers can follow Malcolm by engaging in a sincere search for the truth.

Malcolm X continuously reinvented himself as he learned more and gained life experience. Teachers are often individuals with strong convictions. Therefore, teachers can usefully make an effort to be teachable teachers, open to the idea that they might be wrong. This is challenging for many classroom teachers, since persons in authority often strive to project knowledge and confidence to their students. But growth and change often require confronting classroom strategies and teaching behaviors that have become ineffective, obsolete, or incorrect.

Malcolm's views remain devastatingly relevant sixty years later, as explained by author James McBride in 2020: "Racism has been our Achilles heel for a long time. It's been the cancer that has just been killing us. And now we want to address the problem. I mean, you can't address the cancer until you know you have it."[17]

TEACHING HISTORICAL TRUTH
TO IMPROVE THE FUTURE

In 2018, a new Civil Rights museum and National Memorial for Peace and Justice opened in Montgomery. The memorial honors the legacy of enslaved African Americans, and in particular the victims of racial terror lynchings in the United States. A visit to this monument is profoundly emotional, a window into inexplicable horror. The monument represents lynched African American bodies symbolically with rusted steel rectangles hanging from the ceiling.

As visitors enter, they see a suspended rectangle for each US county where a lynching has taken place: Leflore County, Mississippi, forty-eight reported lynchings; Columbia County, Florida, twenty reported lynchings. The names of the victims are engraved on each steel frame.

Visitors walk through 800 hanging steel commemoratives. The enormity of the number of lynchings that have occurred in our nation, tangible and pervasive, paralyzes many visitors, regardless of race, background, age, or beliefs. The Equal Justice Initiative has documented 4084 racial terror lynchings in twelve Southern states and more than 300 racial terror lynchings in other states between 1877 and 1950.[18] Visitors often start out in conversation but become silent as they make their way through the rusted steel symbols. For many, tears fall. Sadness and remorse are intense and palpable.

The memorial floor descends along a long ramp, causing the hanging steel "bodies" to slowly rise as visitors continue through the exhibit . . . the rectangles are "lynched" using art and architecture, providing an increasingly intense emotional experience. New Hanover County, North Carolina, twenty-two reported lynchings; McClennan County, Texas, fifteen names of lynched African Americans. Some visitors instinctively run their hands over the names, in a desperate, tactile attempt to absorb the horror of our nation's history.

Visitors to the Legacy Memorial represent many nations, races, ethnicities, and life experiences. Most weep at the darkness, hatred, violence, and evil. The shameful history of our forefathers. Malcolm X reminded us that our nation was built on genocide and slavery.

Eddie S. Glaude Jr., the James S. McDonnell Distinguished University Professor of African American Studies at Princeton University, writes eloquently about his 2019 visit to the Legacy Memorial, sharing his personal reactions to the devastating experience, concluding with his belief that our nation needs to begin again: "A new story doesn't mean that we discard all the elements of the old story, nor does it mean that we dwell only on our sins. Instead, we narrate our national beginnings in light of our contradictions and our aspirations. Innocence is left aside."[19]

James Baldwin's brilliant analysis of race included his observation that people of different races had vastly different experiences in the world, and as such had different "systems of reality" that caused them to be unable to comprehend each other.[20]

Our challenge as teachers and as humans is to attempt to remain aware and conscious of our past, even when it is uncomfortable. Children's television host Fred Rogers, studied in chapter 3, said: "Discovering the truth about ourselves is the work of a lifetime, but it is worth the effort."[21] Continuous self-assessment and lifetime learning allow teachers to move forward when confronted with our truths.

Education writer Parker Palmer emphasized the centrality of this idea: "The work required to 'know thyself' is neither selfish nor narcissistic. Whatever self-knowledge we attain as teachers will serve our students and our scholarship well. Good teaching requires self-knowledge."[22] Staying open-minded to ideas, both new and old, provides greater understanding and ability to teach others.

ANGER

Why was Malcolm X so angry? Upon learning how he and his family had been treated by white people, anger seems an appropriate and rational response to the severe racial violence experienced throughout his life. Teachers can use this insight every day: we don't know what has happened in our students' lives. We can make our classrooms more conducive to learning, and along the way, make the world a better place, by striving to help students even if they are disrespectful, question our authority, or disregard classroom rules and procedures.

Teachers can better help students when they learn more about their past, their current situation, and their hopes and dreams for the future. Experienced teachers know how childhood and college experiences enter the learning environment.

At times, students bring a lack of cooperation, or even hostility, to school. This can take place during class, with public confrontations, or privately in conversations with teachers. The life story of Malcolm X offers important guidance in such situations. In many cases, there can be hidden causes of student misbehavior or hostility; something from the student's past or present situation can have a negative impact on behavior, motivation, and teacher relationships.

Anger and frustration often accompany poor performance: it is not uncommon for students to blame teachers for a low grade. Occasionally, outstanding students get angry at missing one point. Earning a 99 percent can cause an intense adverse reaction for some students. Teachers should not be surprised: teachers often blame students for classroom shortcomings.

One student experience is worthy of mention. Kevin was a student of privilege: white, male, and from a high-income family in an affluent suburban neighborhood. Kevin came to the first day of class, and appeared confident, intelligent, and capable. After the first day, however, Kevin did not attend class until the first exam. During the exam, Kevin did not spend time answering questions. Instead, he glared at the instructor, with enormous anger.

The source of Kevin's anger appeared to be the difficulty of the exam, the course, and the instructor. After a few more lectures of Kevin angrily attending class, he stopped coming to class and did not complete any course assignments, exams, or quizzes for the rest of the semester. Emails were sent to Kevin to see if there was anything could be done to help him out. Kevin was given encouragement to complete the class, so he would not have to retake it.

The teacher hoped to find out the actual cause of Kevin's classroom behavior, but was unable to connect or ask him in person. Most teachers spend time worrying about this type of student, concerned that they had personally triggered the poor performance, hostility, or sour relationship. Weeks went by with no insights or answers.

During final exams, a message from the Dean's Office arrived, asking all instructors to please excuse Kevin from course attendance and requirements. Kevin's roommate had died of a drug overdose. Kevin and his roommate had been heavy drug users. In many cases, teachers are surprised with this type of news. Surprised that they did not think of this possibility. They often worry that they did something wrong, internalizing the situation. Other teachers blame the students for lack of discipline, character defects, or lack of effort. Kevin later went to rehab, retook the course, and graduated from college, and successfully started a career.

Malcolm X once said, "Don't be in a hurry to condemn because he doesn't do what you do or think as you think or as fast. There was a time when you didn't know what you know today."[23] Effective teachers move forward with unconditional positive regard for students, in spite of their behaviors, attitudes, or performance. This act of forgiveness is one of the key features of successful teaching. And a successful life. In this sense, educators are like ministers, priests, and other religious leaders. Recall that Malcolm X's father was a Baptist preacher, and Malcolm's own profession was the ministry.

CONCLUSION

The most powerful lesson from Malcolm X is forgiveness: "Since I learned the *truth* in Mecca, my dearest friends have come to include *all* kinds—some Christians, Jews, Buddhists, Hindus, agnostics, and even atheists! . . . My friends today are black, brown, red, yellow and *white*!"[24] If Malcolm could transform his anger into forgiveness, teachers can do it too.

The sooner and more completely we forgive students for their mistakes, errors in judgment, and personality quirks, the better our teaching becomes, and the more effective learning becomes. Forgiveness is no trivial undertaking. Malcolm X once said: "We need more light about each other. Light creates understanding, understanding creates love, love creates patience, and patience creates unity."[25]

Malcolm also provides a powerful lesson in perseverance in the face the difficulty of the teaching task: "Stumbling is not falling."[26] Good teaching requires continuous transformation, constant reflection, and an unfailing commitment to improvement. Sincere effort toward improving teaching content pedagogy, and relationships with students can lead to dramatic student success. When teachers help students, it not only assists them with their current question, but also provides a model for helping others to improve our world. Malcolm X said: "Education is the passport to the future, for tomorrow belongs to those who prepare for it today."[27]

INTERSECTIONS

I always had a deep affection for Malcolm and felt that he had a great ability to put his finger on the existence and the root of the problem. He was an eloquent spokesman for his point of view and no one can honestly doubt that Malcolm had a great concern for the problems we face as a race.

—Martin Luther King, Jr. in a telegram to Betty
Shabazz after Malcolm X's murder[28]

Turning my back on Malcolm was one of the mistakes that I regret most in my life. I wish I'd been able to tell Malcolm I was sorry, that he was right about so many things. But he was killed before I got the chance.

—Muhammad Ali[29]

TEACHING SUMMARY: REINVENT YOUR TEACHING LIKE MALCOLM X

- Preparation. Educate yourself like Malcolm X: learn everything that there is to know about your subject matter. Realize that there is always more to learn.
- Discipline. Try to make every moment of classroom interaction memorable and worthwhile.
- Take time to build a community of learning with acceptance of others. Model it, teach it.
- Conviction. Make your lectures, courses, and interactions with students more timely, relevant, urgent, and clear. Use truth as your guiding principle.
- Transformation. Revelation. Stay open to new ideas. Be a teachable teacher. Recognize when you are wrong. Change when facts change. Replace ineffective practices.
- Forgiveness. Students, teachers, and administrators will disrespect teachers and question our ability and authority. The sooner one can forgive and forget, the better we will be able to fully participate in human relationships. We become better teachers when we forgive.

NOTES

1. Malcolm X Website.
2. Quotefancy, "Malcolm X."
3. Malcolm, X and Haley, *Autobiography*.
4. Lee and Aftab, *Spike Lee*.
5. Greatest Books Website.
6. Malcolm, X and Haley, *Autobiography*, 3.
7. Malcolm, X and Haley, *Autobiography*, 153–154.
8. Malcolm, X and Haley, *Autobiography*, 179.
9. Malcolm X Website.
10. Malcolm X Website.
11. Malcolm X Website.
12. Malcolm X Website.
13. Malcolm, X and Haley, *Autobiography*, 366.
14. Malcolm, X and Haley, *Autobiography*, 429.
15. Malcolm X Website.
16. BrainyQuote, "Malcolm X."
17. Sanders, *McBride*.
18. Equal Justice Initiative Website, *Lynching*.
19. Glaude, "Begin Again."
20. Buccola, *Fire*.
21. Rogers and Junod, *Beautiful Day*, 153.
22. Palmer, *Courage*, 3.
23. Malcolm X Website.
24. Malcolm, X and Haley, *Autobiography*, 375.
25. Malcolm X Website.
26. Malcolm X Website.
27. BrainyQuote, "Malcolm X."
28. Malcolm X Website.
29. Ali and Ali, *Butterfly*.

REFERENCES

Ali, Muhammad and Hana Yasmeen Ali. *The Soul of a Butterfly: Reflections on Life's Journey*. New York: Simon & Schuster, 2004.

Brainyquote. Malcolm X Quotes. Accessed July 23, 2021. https://www.brainyquote .com/authors/malcolm-x-quotes

Buccola, Nicholas. *The Fire Is upon Us: James Baldwin, William F. Buckley Jr., and the Debate over Race in America*. Princeton, NJ: Princeton University Press, 2020.

Equal Justice Initiative Website. *Lynching in America: Confronting the Legacy of Racial Terror*. Accessed June 25, 2020. https://lynchinginamerica.eji.org/about

Glaude, Eddie S. Jr. "We Need to Begin Again: In the Midst of a Moral Reckoning, America Needs a Third Founding." *The Atlantic*, July 18, 2020. Accessed July 23, 2021. https://www.theatlantic.com/ideas/archive/2020/07/why-we-need-begin -again/614326/

Greatest Books Website. Accessed June 18, 2020. https://thegreatestbooks.org/

Lee, Spike, and Aftab, Kaleem. *Spike Lee: That's My Story and I'm Sticking to It.* New York: Norton, 2006.

Malcolm X Website. Accessed June 18, 2020. https://www.malcolmx.com/

Malcolm, X., and Haley, Alex. *The Autobiography of Malcolm X as Told to Alex Haley.* New York: Ballantine, 1992.

Palmer, Parker J. *The Courage to Teach.* San Francisco, CA: Jossey-Bass Publishers, 1998.

Quotefancy. "Malcolm X Quotes." Accessed July 23, 2021. https://quotefancy.com /quote/859169/Malcolm-X-I-want-to-be-remembered-as-someone-who-was-sin -cere-Even-if-I-made-mistakes-they

Rogers, Fred and Tom Junod. *A Beautiful Day in the Neighborhood: Neighborly Words of Wisdom from Mister Rogers.* New York: Penguin, 2019.

Sanders, Sam. Interview: "Author James McBride Sees Hope in Recent Activism for Racial Justice." *National Public Radio. Morning Edition*, June 24, 2020. Accessed June 29, 2020. https://www.npr.org/2020/06/24/882678420/author-james-mcbride -sees-hope-in-recent-activism-for-racial-justice

Chapter 6

Success under Extreme Conditions

Albert Camus

Figure 6.1   Albert Camus. *Source*: Wikimedia Commons. Robert Edwards.

In the midst of winter, I found there was, within me, an invincible summer.

—Albert Camus[1]

What we learn in times of pestilence: that there are more things to admire in men than to despise.

—Albert Camus[2]

CHAPTER SYNOPSIS

Powerful lessons for teaching are gleaned from philosopher and writer Albert Camus' search for light in dark times. His solution to the absurdity of life is humanity, decency, and good sense. Camus' nonfiction work *The Myth of Sisyphus* and novel *The Plague* provide useful insights for teaching during challenging times, and guidance for when teaching becomes routine or unforgiving. Teachers are bolstered by Camus' insistence that life is worth living in spite of personal, bureaucratic, and interpersonal challenges. Specific actions for teaching under challenging circumstances are outlined and discussed.

Albert Camus (1913–1960) was a French writer and philosopher, dedicated to uncovering truth and solving real problems. Camus devoted his life to clear thinking about the most important threats to humankind: violence, totalitarianism, injustice, anxiety, and the absurdity of the human condition. After a childhood in Algeria, Camus began his influential career in the midst of the Nazi occupation of France during World War II.

Camus joined the French Resistance as a journalist and editor of *Combat*, a banned newspaper that opposed the Nazi oppressors. Given the danger of his work, Camus used a pseudonym and false identification to avoid capture. Camus' life work was strongly influenced by his close experience with the Nazi's capture, murder, and torture of innocent civilians. Men, women, and children were brutally killed for their political views, ethnic origin, physical or mental limitations, or sexuality.

Throughout his writing career, Camus' focus was on a lack of ability to understand suffering, violence, and the purpose of life. Yet, after personal struggle, poor health from tuberculosis, conflict with family and friends, and close observation of genocide, Camus rejected negativity and actively revolted against the absurdity of life. Camus' optimistic conclusion is a common theme in his clear, interesting, and meaningful novels, essays, and plays. Camus' ability to capture the reader's attention led to a Nobel Prize in Literature in 1957.

Two of Camus' most famous works are a philosophical essay *The Myth of Sisyphus* (1942) and a novel *The Plague* (1947). *Sisyphus* concerns the human desire for meaning, and *The Plague* investigates the impact of a deadly bubonic plague on a coastal North African city. These books, written over seven decades ago, remain astonishingly accurate contemporary guidebooks for teaching under challenging conditions. Camus' universal and eternal ideas provide assistance to teachers when they need it most: under unpredicted and extraordinary circumstances.

THE MYTH OF SISYPHUS

During the Nazi occupation, Camus began thinking about "whether life has a meaning." This exploration became *The Myth of Sisyphus*, originally published in 1942.[3] In spite of the war, Camus reached a positive, life-affirming conclusion: "Although 'The Myth of Sisyphus' poses mortal problems, it sums itself up for me as a lucid invitation to live and to create, in the very midst of the desert."[4]

Camus believed that humans have a strong desire for the world to be reasonable and rational. This innate desire to understand the world is particularly strong when confronted with difficulty, evil, or suffering. Sadly, there are no answers or solutions to the quest for meaning.

Camus defined "the absurd" as this fundamental conflict between what we want from the universe (meaning, order, reasons) and what we find in the universe (lack of understanding, formless chaos). In Camus' words, "The absurd is born of this confrontation between the human need and the unreasonable silence of the world."[5] The absurdity of life is inescapable for Camus, a conclusion that could lead to despair. Camus suggests that if we confront life's absurdity and accept it, we can move forward by actively and insistently rebelling against the absurd and rejecting the morosity of life.

Camus communicates his philosophy through the Greek legend of Sisyphus. According to Homer, Sisyphus was a wise mortal, the founder and first king of Corinth.[6] Sisyphus was "The most cunning of men," who cheated death twice and, as a result, angered the gods.[7] In his first death experience, Sisyphus died and descended to Hades, where he captured the god of death, Thanatos. Sisyphus placed Thanatos (death) in chains so that no mortal humans would ever die again. The gods were not happy; Ares, the god of war, intervened by freeing Death, causing life and mortality to return on earth.

After dying a second time, Sisyphus returned to the underworld, where he encountered the god of death, Hades, and his wife Persephone. Sisyphus, the clever one, negotiated with Persephone to be briefly returned to earth and the realm of the living. Sisyphus argued that he would convince his wife on earth to perform required rituals for the dead, then immediately return to Hades. Sisyphus was allowed to return to earth, where he stayed, violating his agreement with Persephone to return to the underworld, and defying death a second time.

Sisyphus' love of life and unwillingness to die angered the gods. When Sisyphus died a third time, Zeus, king of the gods, concocted an eternal, tedious punishment for Sisyphus. Homer describes the tortuous penalty: "he wrestled with a huge rock with both hands. Bracing himself and thrusting with hands and feet he pushed the boulder uphill to the top. But every time, as he was about to send it toppling over the crest, its sheer weight turned it back, and once again towards the plain the pitiless rock rolled down."[8] This physical, mental, and emotional humiliation occurred daily.

Sisyphus is tasked with struggling purposefully, but with neither success nor hope, a perfect example of the absurd. Into this hopeless and repetitive struggle, Camus declares that "Sisyphus is the absurd hero."[9] Camus describes in detail the toil and sweat of Sisyphus pushing the rock up the hill, and the glorious feeling of attaining daily victory each time the stone reaches the summit.

Camus describes how Sisyphus must feel as he watches helplessly when the stone rolls back down the hill: "At each of those moments when he leaves the heights and gradually sinks toward the lairs of the gods, he is superior to his fate. He is stronger than the rock."[10]

Camus concludes that happiness is a natural outcome of the absurd: "The struggle itself toward the heights is enough to fill a man's heart. One must imagine Sisyphus happy."[11] Education scholar Mordechai Gordon emphasizes the importance of Sisyphus for teaching: "Camus insisted that, as a tragic hero, Sisyphus should be revered for his rebellious attitude and for not giving in to cynicism and despair in the face of his awful predicament. Indeed, Camus argued that we [teachers] should regard Sisyphus as a model."[12]

Gordon considers teaching to be an absurd profession: "one that faces numerous obstacles and challenges and continually falls short of its intended goals."[13] Sisyphus is an absurd hero because he recognizes the absurdity of his terrible punishment, accepts his situation, and cheerfully rebels against his fate. Teachers can do the same.

Teachers recognize "the absurd" in Camus' essay. Teaching is interpersonal; relational; social; and public. Teachers are committed to helping others by providing knowledge and skills that will improve their students' lives. At times, this strong desire to serve others can be met with indifference. Even worse, it can trigger hostility from students who struggle with authority, substance abuse, financial challenges, health issues, learning disabilities, or other hardships.

Some students exhibit a diabolically rebellious attitude against learning, studying, relating, or succeeding. A teacher's well-intended efforts can backfire. The pain of student rejection can sting, particularly after genuine, sustained efforts to assist.

College instructors may face reduced class attendance, lack of class participation, or lonely office hours. Teachers of young children may deal with inattention, disruptive behavior, or lack of effort. Teaching is difficult, because it is personal and interpersonal. A teacher's identity and self-image centers on the ability to help others. Sharing knowledge and their lives with others causes teachers to be vulnerable. Kindness, sincerity, and good faith effort will be rejected by some students, at least some of the time.

Teachers not only recognize "the absurd," but they are also familiar with the "absurd hero." The absurd hero is the teacher who continues trying against all odds; the teacher who forgives and forgets student misbehaviors; the teacher who moves forward with effort, enthusiasm, and knowledge; the teacher who does not give up until each challenged student turns things around to learn and achieve success. The absurd teaching hero is . . . every committed teacher!

THE PLAGUE

After living through the German occupation of France during World War II, Camus planned a book about the Nazi horror. Camus' *The Plague* is a detailed description of a pandemic, and how a group of people struggle against the bubonic plague in Oran, a coastal city in North Africa. Camus catalogs a wide range of emotional responses to the disease, the lockdown of the city, and the death of a large proportion of the city's population. The book is also an allegory for fascism, and how citizens react to the rise of a dictator, totalitarianism, and violence used against innocent civilians.

Camus sets the scene in Oran: "For the most part they were men with well-defined and sound ideas on everything concerning exports, banking, the fruit or wine trade; men of proved ability in handling problems relating to insurance, the interpretation of ill-drawn contracts, and the like. . . . But as regards plague their competence was practically nil."[14] Steve Coll, a journalist, academic, and business executive adds: "That Camus, writing in the mid-nineteen-forties, could conjure with such clarity, during an epidemic, a political morality that advocates for factual reporting, medical science, and public-health regimens seems astonishing."[15]

Camus uncannily describes panicked buying of goods when fake news is spread of their curative or preventative value; authorities' attempt to minimize the epidemic; the imperfect development of a vaccine; high mortality rates in the city jails; exhausted health workers; and the monotony and isolation of the quarantine.[16] Social critic Liesl Schillinger summarizes,

"Although his novel tracks the progression of a specific epidemic in a specific city, country, and time frame, Camus' true subject lies outside of time and place."[17]

Camus carefully documents the impact of the pandemic: "a feeling normally as individual as the ache of separation from those one loves suddenly became a feeling in which all shared alike, and—together with fear—the greatest affliction of the long period of exile that lay ahead."[18] Schillinger describes the heavy emotional toll of Camus' plague and the Covid-19 experience: "feelings of isolation, fear, and loss of agency."[19]

Camus also captured a feature of contagions: "the frantic desire for life that thrives in the heart of every great calamity."[20] Those who have experienced quarantine or isolation recognize this deep yearning for community, interrelationships, and social interaction. The isolation of Oran's quarantine and lockdown result in pandemic fatigue, causing many citizens to rebel against rules put in place to subdue the disease.

The plague transforms each of Camus' central characters, and these changes become a major theme of the book. Camus describes what happens to different personality types when confronted with both personal and collective adversity. Camus' plague is highly contagious, causing a conflict between each citizen's desire to preserve their own life, and do what is right for the city as a whole. Is our duty individual or societal? How do we achieve the appropriate balance between self-care and care for others?

Theologian Wessel Bentley captures the eerie likeness between Camus' citizens of Oran and people throughout the world under Covid-19: "As people deal with their new reality, some are found to be in denial, some rebel against the strict social measures, some simply accept their state of being, whilst others deliberately fight the scourge of disease by caring for the stricken."[21] The contagion experience changes two characters: Dr. Rieux, a medical doctor, and Father Paneloux, a priest. Both the doctor and the priest move from positions of certainty to doubt.

Camus concludes that the disease will always be with us, referring to both the plague and the fascism's attractiveness to some individuals and groups. Camus suggests that both natural and political calamities have their root in human failure. Efforts to combat the disease are ineffective, and a deep weariness and disillusionment settle into the daily life of the citizens of Oran. Political dissident and humanitarian Vaclav Havel stated, "Modern man must descend the spiral of his own absurdity to the lowest point: only then can he look beyond it."[22]

Camus' great lesson for teachers is to carry on, to persevere, to remain enthusiastic in the face of complexity and obstacles. Teaching is difficult, and Camus' notion of the absurd suggests that teaching will always be difficult. Once Camus' fictional plague is over, the city of Oran erupts in jubilation.

Rieux, however, has learned that "such joy is always imperiled . . . the plague bacillus never dies or disappears for good."[23] Humans will always suffer from health, relational, and political challenges. Teachers will always face enormous challenges in achieving and maintaining effectiveness.

A teacher's goal is to share knowledge with others. We are limited in our ability to do this. Camus recommends facing teaching challenges squarely, by never letting our guard down. Watch for potential problems that might arise. Try to proactively stop the problem before it spreads, grows, or festers. Most teachers strongly desire to make a positive impact on the life of a student. Students have a strong desire to learn, to succeed, to be affirmed for who they are. Successful teaching requires acceptance of the absurd to enhance student knowledge, and thereby improve the world.

When Camus won the Nobel Prize in Literature in 1957, he immediately wrote a letter to his childhood teacher, Monsieur Germain: "Without you, without the affectionate hand you extended to the small poor child that I was, without your teaching and example, none of all this would have happened . . . your efforts, your work, and the generous heart you put into it still live in one of your little schoolboys who, despite the years, has never stopped being your grateful pupil. I embrace you with all my heart."[24]

TEACHING UNDER CHALLENGING CIRCUMSTANCES

Professor Steve Coll proposes that, "Camus was less interested in the evolving science of epidemic response than in our capacity as individuals to face the truth, endure, and contribute to success under extreme conditions."[25] Education was disrupted during spring of 2020 when the Coronavirus spread across the globe. The disorder in teacher and student lives resulted in the transformation of teaching and learning. Students and their families were sick; some lost relatives to the disease. Most students, from preschool through graduate school, were living and learning remotely, totally dependent on the Internet for education, relation, and information.

As Camus described the mental, physical, and emotional exhaustion caused by the bubonic plague in Oran, a major outcome of the 2020 coronavirus outbreak was stress and anxiety. Sources of anxiety during tense events can include both traditional sources of academic stress, but also the stress of online learning, at-home schooling, general uncertainty, health and safety, and financial difficulty.[26]

Camus' characters in *The Plague* suggest two goals for when darkness prevails: (1) clarity, and (2) action. A major theme of *The Plague* is a call for plain, clear language, simple language, and transparent communication. Jean

Tarrou concludes that "All of our troubles arise from our failure to use plain, clear-cut language."[27] This is a major challenge for health authorities during a pandemic. Teachers can use simple language to make their lessons, goals, and expectations clear.

Doctor Rieux faces the absurd, and chooses action. He discovers that his best course of action is to let go of speculation, rumors, and theories, and instead focus on the "certitudes" of his performing medical rounds.[28] "It was only a matter of lucidly recognizing what had to be recognized; of dispelling extraneous shadows and doing what needs to be done . . . the thing was to do your job as it should be done."[29] Teachers who choose action can, like Rieux, make the best out of a challenging situation.

Learning is maximized when the level of challenge is in line with the level of student readiness. Too much anxiety causes students to shut down; too little results in indifference, boredom, and lack of effort. When stress levels are high, and anxiety is severe among a large proportion of students, teachers can adjust their teaching style to better match student needs. When students have high levels of anxiety, typical classroom assignments, exams, and pedagogies may increase stress and reduce learning. Classroom behavior and class assignments can be productively redesigned to accommodate student needs under challenging conditions.

Extravagant mercy can be useful in times of high stress and anxiety. Deadlines can be extended; missed deadlines forgiven; excuses accepted. Inexhaustible flexibility may go against many teachers' intuition of what is best for students. After all, an important goal of education is learning the importance of timeliness, punctuality, and meeting deadlines. However, during a crisis or unprecedented time, flexibility may be more effective, and in some situations, a mandatory prerequisite to achieve teaching and learning.

As Covid-19 spread during spring 2020, schools, colleges, and universities rapidly moved to online learning. Administrators advised instructors to be accommodating to student needs, recommending complete forgiveness. Many teachers realized gains in effectiveness by transitioning from a rigid, "old-school" approach to a more student-centered teaching method.

Rapid response to student queries and concerns is an important component of effective instruction, and becomes essential during challenging circumstances. Teachers who are "hyper-responsive" to all student communication demonstrate their desire to help students learn, and as a result, receive more respect and achieve greater levels of student learning.

Teachers can also increase the frequency of communication to assist student engagement. When face-to-face interactions are not possible, online communication can cause students to feel more connected with the class and the instructor. Care and support can make a positive difference for many students.

When possible, grading can be based on multiple attempts, rather than a single grade with no opportunity for improvement. The loss of focus associated with higher stress levels causes learning to be more likely to occur in smaller increments. All features of a course can be divided into smaller parts to accommodate shorter attention spans: long lectures can be recorded in multiple short videos; exams can be configured as multiple, "smaller stakes" instruments to replace one long exam; assignment, reports, and papers can all be usefully modified.

Written assignments can be completed over several graded assignments: research question, thesis statement, sources, draft, final paper, and revision. Students under pressure often benefit enormously when action is taken to reduce the length of lectures and course assessments. Second chances to learn can turn a class from an anxiety-provoking experience into an effective, rewarding one.

CONCLUSION

Teachers can use extravagant mercy, inexhaustible flexibility, complete forgiveness, and hyper-responsiveness, and frequent caring communication to achieve higher levels of learning during periods of elevated anxiety. By providing students with opportunities for growth and continued improvement, a teacher can become an absurd hero by turning a difficult and challenging situation into a positive, productive learning environment.

Elaine Smokewood was a fifty-four-year-old English professor at Oklahoma City University when she began to lose her ability to speak due to Lou Gehrig's disease.[30] She was surprised to learn that she was able to teach more effectively by changing her teaching style from lecturing to listening. Smokewood reported that if she listened to students carefully, thoughtfully, generously, and nonjudgmentally, the students would impress her with the complexity of their thinking, the depth of their insight, humor, compassion, wisdom, and honesty. Smokewood is an absurd teaching hero.

When teachers strive to enhance their care and concern for students, they often experience enhanced outcomes, positive interactions, a more productive classroom environment, greater student engagement, and better performance on class assessments. Camus summarized the absurd teaching hero: "Greatness consists in trying to be great. There is no other way."[31]

INTERSECTIONS

Albert Camus and Martin Luther King Jr are two first class role models who lived out their passion for justice and freedom. Today, they are

*among the heroes who are well remembered around the world. The
following words seem appropriate to reflect what they stood for: "For
all who have sought to make a difference in the lives of men by their
service and life, and to lighten the dark places of the earth."*

—Carl E. Moyler[32]

*Like Camus and his Dr. Rieux, Dylan has to embrace the sadness of his
days in order to come out the other side in a search for meaning and a
kind of immortality.*

—*Ed Siegel, reviewing Bob Dylan's 39th studio album,
"Rough and Rowdy Ways," released June 19, 2020.*[33]

TEACHING SUMMARY: TEACH IN
CHALLENGING CONDITIONS LIKE CAMUS

- Recognize *the absurd* in teaching (the conflict between the desire for meaning and the inability to find answers).
- Respond to *the absurd* by becoming an *absurd teaching hero*, continuing to strive for excellence in spite of difficulties or lack of understanding.
- Be humble about how much we know; accept that there is much that we do not know.
- Recognize when levels of anxiety are elevated.
- Create a classroom environment by first meeting students' basic needs of safety and self-esteem, so that learning can then take place.
- Reduce the length of lectures, assignments, reading, and assessments by dividing them into smaller parts.
- Maintain a high level of organization, clarity, and transparency.
- Practice extravagant mercy, inexhaustible flexibility, complete forgiveness, and hyper-responsiveness. Do not lower expectations, rigor, or standards in the process.
- Increase the frequency of communication and expressions of care and support.

NOTES

1. Camus, *Tipasa*, 171.
2. Camus, *Plague*, 297.
3. Camus, *Sisyphus*, Preface.
4. Camus, *Sisyphus*, Preface.

5. Camus, *Sisyphus*, 28.
6. Homer, *Iliad*.
7. Homer, *Iliad*.
8. Homer, *Odyssey*, Book 11, line 593.
9. Camus, *Sisyphus*, 120.
10. Camus, *Sisyphus*, 121.
11. Camus, *Sisyphus*, 123.
12. Gordon, *Teachers*.
13. Gordon, *Teachers*.
14. Camus, *Plague*, 102.
15. Coll, *Political Tests*.
16. Theroux, *End of Coronavirus*.
17. Schillinger, *Learn*.
18. Camus, *Plague*, 63.
19. Schillinger, *Learn*.
20. Camus, *Plague*, 115.
21. Bentley, *Reflections*, 2.
22. Havel and Huizdala, *Disturbing*.
23. Camus, *Plague*, 297.
24. Popova, *Beautiful Letter*.
25. Coll, *Political Tests*.
26. Brown et al., *Anxiety*.
27. Camus, *Plague*, 243.
28. Coll, *Political Tests*.
29. Camus, *Plague*, 39.
30. Young, *Terrible Disease*.
31. Camus, *Notebooks: 1942-1951*.
32. Moyler, *On Freedom*, Acknowledgements. The quote is an inscription on the wall of the Civil Rights Museum, 16th street, Birmingham, Alabama, USA, author unknown.
33. Siegel, *From Camus*.

REFERENCES

Bentley, W. "Reflections on the Characters of Dr. Rieux and Fr Paneloux in Camus' The Plague in a Consideration of Human Suffering During the COVID-19 Pandemic." *HTS Teologiese Studies/Theological Studies* 76, no. 4 (2020): a6087. doi: 10.4102/hts.v76i4.6087

Brown, Roger, Steve Buck, Michelle Kibler, Jerrod Penn, and Na Zuo. "Course-Related Student Anxiety during COVID-19: A Problem and Some Solutions." *Applied Economics Teaching Resources* 3, no. 1 (March 2021): 1–21.

Camus, Albert. *Notebooks: 1942–1951*. New York: Houghton Mifflin Harcourt, 1965.

Camus, Albert. "Return to Tipasa," from *Summer* (1954). In *Lyrical and Critical Essays*, edited by Philip Thody, translated by Ellen Kennedy, 162–171. New York: Knopf, 1968.

Camus, Albert. *The Myth of Sisyphus*. Originally published in French as *Le Mythe de Sisyphe* (1942). Translated by Justin O'Brien. New York: Vintage International, 2018.

Camus, Albert. *The Plague*. Originally published in French as *La Peste* (1947). Translated by Stuart Gilbert. New York: Vintage, 1991.

Coll, Steve. "Camus and the Political Tests of a Pandemic." *The New Yorker*, May 19, 2020. https://www.newyorker.com/news/daily-comment/camus-and-the-political-tests-of-a-pandemic

Gordon, Mordechai. "Teachers as Absurd Heroes: Camus' Sisyphus and the Promise of Rebellion," *Educational Philosophy and Theory* 48, no. 6 (May 2016): 589–604. doi: 10.1080/00131857.2015.1058219.

Havel, Vaclav, and Karel Huizdala. *Disturbing the Peace: A Conversation with Karel Huizdala*. New York: Vintage, 1986.

Homer. *The Iliad*. Translated by Robert Fagles. Ann Arbor, MI: University of Michigan Press, 2007.

Homer. *The Odyssey*. Translated by Robert Fagles. London: Penguin, 1997.

Moyler, Carl E. *On Freedom and Revolt: A Comparative Investigation*. San Diego, CA: ReadersMagnet, 2018.

Popova, Maria. "Albert Camus's Beautiful Letter of Gratitude to His Childhood Teacher after Winning the Nobel Prize." *BrainPickings*, November 19, 2014. Accessed April 2, 2021. https://www.brainpickings.org/2014/11/19/albert-camus-letter-teacher/

Schillinger, Liesl. "What We Can Learn (and Should Unlearn) from Albert Camus's *The Plague*: Liesl Schillinger on Catastrophe, Contagion, and the Human Condition." *Literary Hub*, March 13, 2020. Accessed March 31, 2021. https://lithub.com/what-we-can-learn-and-should-unlearn-from-albert-camuss-the-plague/

Siegel, Ed. "From Camus' 'The Plague' To Dylan's 'Rough and Rowdy Ways,' Sad Is the New Happy." *Wbur*, July 29, 2020. Accessed April 7, 2021. https://www.wbur.org/artery/2020/07/29/dylan-camus-globe-commentary

Theroux, Marcel. "The End of Coronavirus: What Plague Literature Tells Us about Our Future." *The Guardian*, May 1, 2020. Accessed March 31, 2021. https://www.theguardian.com/books/2020/may/01/the-end-of-coronavirus-what-plague-literature-tells-us-about-our-future

Young, J.R. "Taught by a Terrible Disease." *The Chronicle of Higher Education*, January 3, 2010. Accessed April 8, 2021. https://www.chronicle.com/article/taught-by-a-terrible-disease/

Zaretsky, Robert. *Albert Camus: Elements of a Life*. Ithaca, NY: Cornell University Press, 2010.

Zaretsky, Robert. *A Life Worth Living: Albert Camus and the Quest for Meaning*. Cambridge, MA: Belknap, 2016.

Chapter 7

Dignity under Duress

Chief Joseph

Figure 7.1 Chief Joseph. *Source*: Wikimedia Commons. File: US Army 52026 An Honorable Leader.jpg

It does not require many words to speak the truth.

—Chief Joseph[1]

Treat all men alike. Give them the same law. Give them an even chance to live and grow.

—Chief Joseph[2]

CHAPTER SYNOPSIS

This chapter highlights student-teacher relationships and our sense of place. The Nimiipuu (Nez Perce) people were forcibly removed from their ancestral home in the Northwest United States, one of the most beautiful and resource-rich areas in the world. White settlers, gold miners, and government officials encroached on this land, resulting in violence and war. Throughout, Chief Joseph retained dignity, grace, and kindness, providing timely lessons for college teachers. Nez Perce history is used to highlight the role of respect in education.

The Nimiipuu (Nez Perce) people originally lived in a large, beautiful region that included present-day north-central Idaho, northeastern Oregon, and southeastern Washington. The Nimiipuu lived in this area between the Bitterroot Mountains to the east and the Blue and Wallowa Mountains to the west for over 11,500 years. This territory includes some of the most remote, wild, and scenic country in the United States. The Nimiipuu ancestral home is the foundation of the tribe's spirituality, culture, and religion.

Beginning in 1850, an increasing number of white settlers arrived in the region to trap, farm, and ranch. Gold was discovered in 1860, causing a rapid influx of miners, and development of boomtowns. Treaties with the United States Government were signed in 1855 and 1863 to force the Nimiipuu onto a reservation at Lapwai, Idaho, reducing their traditional homeland by over 90 percent.

The treaties resulted in a major division between the Nimiipuu peoples. Early in the white settlement era, the Nimiipuu welcomed Missionaries to their land, and many converted to Christianity. This group was called the "treaty band" of the Nimiipuu. As settlers became more numerous, a "nontreaty band" grew, called the Too-ats. This oppositional group followed a new religious movement (the Dreamers) who shunned white ways of farming and Christianity.[3]

By 1876, a majority of Nimiipuu had moved to the reservation. Increasing tensions between the white settlers and the nontreaty natives caused the US government to send Civil War Veteran General Oliver Otis Howard and the US Army to the area with orders to force the noncompliant Nimiipuu onto the reservation.

In June 1877, violence broke out, and approximately 750 men, women, and children of the nontreaty band avoided military confrontation by fleeing the area. In an epic retreat, this group kept the US Army at bay for over 1500 miles and 15 weeks, in the attempt to get to freedom in Canada. The group suffered enormous losses.

On October 5, 1877, less than 50 miles from the safety of the Canadian border, the remaining Nimiipuu agreed to a truce. Chief Joseph made his famous surrender speech, "From where the sun now stands, I will fight no more forever."[4] Joseph and his followers were promised that they could return to their original homeland in exchange for peace.

Once the Nimiipuu surrendered their weapons, however, they were removed to Fort Leavenworth in Kansas, and later forced into exile in the Oklahoma Indian Territory. The Nimiipuu spent nearly seven years in what they called Eeikish Pah (the Hot Place), where their numbers diminished due to mistreatment, disease, and relocation. In 1885, Chief Joseph and his band were allowed to return to the Pacific Northwest. Even then, the group was forced to live on the Colville reservation in Washington State, rather than their homeland in the Wallowa Valley (the Land of Winding Waters) in Northeastern Oregon.

Chief Joseph is considered by many of his contemporaries and present-day historians alike to be an exceptional chief, leader, and diplomat. Educators can find much to emulate in Joseph's leadership: kindness, honesty, and generosity. Western photographer Edward Curtis reported, "I think he was one of the greatest men who ever lived."[5]

Chief Joseph is considered to have been a deeply honorable man, even in the face of settlers taking his homeland away and repeated broken promises of the US government. The antagonism between the Nimiipuu and whites was emotionally charged due to a long history of peace and mutual respect between the natives and white settlers. Joseph recalled, "All the Nez Perces made friends with Lewis and Clark, and agreed to let them pass through their country and never to make war on white men. This promise the Nez Perce have never broken."[6]

Biographer Helen Howard writes of Joseph, "His story is the tragic and epic struggle of the American Indians who were relentlessly, fraudulently, and treacherously dispossessed of their hunting, fishing, and grazing grounds to satisfy the white man's greed for more land."[7] Educators can gain enormously from the story of Joseph, the diplomatic hero who used his knowledge to build effective relationships with the Nimiipuu, other tribes, and white leaders.

A STUDENT-TEACHER INTERACTION

Finnish educator Aino-Maija Lahtinen asserts, "The most basic aspect of teaching at all levels is the building of interpersonal relationships with students."[8] The following story describes an interaction between a student Paul and his teacher, highlighting the complexity of relationships between teachers and students. Paul was intelligent, interesting, and interested. A pleasure to be around and to have in class, Paul did well during the first several weeks of the semester. He came to office hours, along with a group of other students.

Paul is a truly likable individual: hard working, friendly, and successful. On his first office visit, Paul shared where he was from: Wichita, Kansas. This small piece of information provided a powerful opening for conversation, and the ability to begin to build a bond with a student. Students often appreciate the opportunity to talk about their hometown, their family, and their sense of place in the world.

"Wichita . . . great place! Is Boeing still hiring workers for the new aircraft project? Which part of town do you live in? North of downtown? That is a nice area." So it went with Paul, who was personable, quick-minded, and a great communicator. His eyes sparkled when he shared information about his family, hometown, and college experience. Paul was also good with other students. During group sessions, he related well with others, explained course content that others did not understand.

Paul earned an "A" on the first exam and felt confident about the course. The second exam resulted in a very low grade for Paul. After receiving his graded exam back during class, Paul appeared during office hours later on the same day. He was unhappy. His comments were part threat (how can you give an exam that half of the class fails?), part fault finding (I didn't answer that question because there wasn't enough space, so I didn't know that I was supposed to answer it!), and part raw, unadulterated emotion (totally unfair!).

Experienced teachers will smile with recognition of this type of conversation . . . but with a pit in their stomachs, knowing that they will face similar conversations again in the future. This situation is not common, but also not uncommon in today's classrooms. Lahtinen concluded: "The most obvious negative feelings seem to be evoked in the teacher when students express directly and in a hostile and aggressive way resentment due to their disappointment about assessment, grading, and problems in learning."[9]

The instructor slowly and carefully explained to Paul what he had missed on the exam, and why, in a measured tone. The exam was checked carefully to find any grading mistakes, with Paul arguing strongly for the correctness of his responses. As he stood up to leave, Paul commented, "I am not trying to be rude or disrespectful." Strangely, that is exactly what he was.

Many features of Paul's interaction are fascinating. How could such a nice person, someone who had built a solid relationship with the teacher, be so angry? Where did the emotion come from? How could he not understand that his poor performance was due to a lack of preparation, particularly since the exam questions were provided to the students, and the average student exam performance was very good? What should be done to keep Paul engaged in the course, both during the unexpected, momentous conversation, and after?

What could be done to avoid or minimize this type of unsettling conversation/outburst/diatribe in the future?

The experiences of Chief Joseph provide help. Momaday exclaims, "He [Chief Joseph] was always a peacemaker. And Lord knows he was provoked. Another kind of man could not have remained in control of himself, in possession of himself. And one of Joseph's great characteristics is that he was always in possession of himself."[10] Lahtinen reminds us that a teacher feels responsible for directing the activities of others to achieve learning objectives. As a result, there is always power and authority in the teacher's actions.[11]

The power dynamics of student-teacher relationships are complex and unique. In most traditional educational settings, the teacher is the authority figure and has more power than the student. However, teachers can learn a great deal from those who are not in power such as Chief Joseph, who was overpowered by the white settlers and ultimately by the US Army. Teachers, and other individuals in authority positions can often improve outcomes by sincere consideration of those who are relatively less powerful in any social, educational, or work interaction.

Lahtinen emphasizes that learning is complex and dynamic: "Pedagogical interaction is lively in nature. The teacher cannot plan teaching in detail or fully control it and the teachers thinking during the interaction is largely intuitive, creative, impulsive, spontaneous, and impulsive in nature."[12]

One cause of Paul's reaction was likely to be his previous academic success. Paul was smart, and he had learned how to transform his intelligence into good grades. However, this exam had essay questions that required a high degree of critical thinking. To achieve a high grade, the course material must be known well, and studying is mandatory, even for the best students. The rigor of the course required more effort than Paul had previously needed to earn the desired grade. The threat of challenging, rigorous exams combined with poor preparation caused Paul's poor grade, and adverse reaction.

As the course progressed, the relationship between student and teacher recovered, and Paul re-engaged in the class, due to the foundational relationship built early in the course during office hours. Building a relationship is not only pleasurable as a social activity; it can also minimize costs of disruption and unhappiness when difficulties arise. Challenges are inevitable in teaching environments. When students and teachers have a solid relationship, they can weather the storms of teaching and learning more effectively.

SENSE OF PLACE

Land was the most important thing for the Nimiipuu; it was their religion. For Chief Joseph (also called, "Young Joseph"), the Wallowa Valley (Land of the

Winding Waters) in northeast Oregon was vital, as it was where his father Tuekakas (Old Joseph), had lived and died. Before he died, Tuekakas told his son to never sell the bones of his father and mother. Chief Joseph never sold the region, but instead was forced out by the US government.

As with Joseph, an individual's home is often important to them. Educators can use the primacy of "home" to begin relationships with students and solidify the relationships over time. By learning as much as possible about students, teachers can solidify the bond with pupils. Lahtinen says, "learning itself is a dynamic and multifaceted phenomenon, comprising simultaneously a cognitive, emotional and psychodynamic as well as social and societal dimension."[13] The emotions that occur when sharing memories of home often connect people. Joseph was a "connector," linking knowledge with people's interests. Teachers can do this, too.

This geographic approach for building relationships can be an effective ice breaker, particularly for shy or quiet educators. Getting people to talk about themselves often results not only in interesting discussions but also in new friendships.

WATKUESE AND LEWIS AND CLARK

Nez Perce tribal member Otis Halfmoon provides perspective on the initial meeting of Lewis and Clark and the Nimiipuu: "they said they 'discovered' my people. In actuality, the Nez Perce people . . . we knew where we were. . . . We discovered Lewis and Clark. Those were the ones that were lost."[14] The story of the Nimiipuu woman Watkuese demonstrates how good relationships can yield good outcomes. Watkuese's name means "lost and was found," or "went away but returned." The Nimiipuu had peace, respect, and good relations with white people for a long period of time, directly due to Watkuese.

In the 1760s or 1770s, the enemy Blackfoot tribe raided the Nimiipuu and stole Watkuese, a young girl at the time. She was raised as a slave and abused by the Blackfeet. She was later traded to a tribe further east, probably near the Red River.[15] There, a white family purchased her from the Blackfeet, treated her well, and with great respect.

Watkuese had a child, yet strongly desired to return to her homeland and family. She escaped with her infant, and survived the long, perilous trek over the Bitterroot Mountains to Nimiipuu land. Her infant died along the way. Upon arrival at home, Watkuese shared stories of the kindness and respect of the Soyapo (white people).

In 1805, Lewis and Clark led the Corps of Discovery in search of the "Northwest Passage," a route from the Mississippi River to the Pacific

Ocean. The group included twenty-eight white men, one African American slave named York, and two Shoshone guides. On September 30, 1805, the Corps came down out of the Rocky Mountains and appeared near a Nimiipuu village, exhausted and near starvation. The young Nimiipuu warriors were suspicious of the group; they had not seen white people before. The Soyapos' facial hair was foreign and mysterious to them, and their guides were Shoshone: a traditional enemy of the Nimiipuu.

The warriors were set on killing the entire Corps of Discovery. This could have been easily accomplished given the weakened state of the expeditionary force after a long mountain pass with little food. Watkuese, now an older woman, heard about the new arrivals, and strongly declared to the warriors, "Do them no harm." Watkuese explained that the Soyapo had treated her well as a slave, and should be taken care of, fed, and treated well.[16]

Lewis and Clark were shown elaborate and extensive hospitality by the Nimiipuu. The company stayed for twenty days, gaining strength from the salmon and camas root provided to them by their generous hosts. The Nimiipuu taught Lewis and Clark about the region; how to get to the Pacific Ocean by following the Snake and Columbia Rivers, and how to construct dugout canoes from Lodgepole Pines. The stay was enormously successful for the Corps of Discovery.

Lewis described the Nimiipuu as "the most hospitable, honest, sincere people that we have met with in our voyage."[17] The good treatment and respect shown to Watkuese by white people many decades before and many miles away resulted in the survival and success of the Lewis and Clark expedition. Teachers can learn a simple, obvious lesson from Nimiipuu history: good relationships yield positive results, particularly when under duress.

The Corps of Discovery's mission included diplomacy with all natives along their route. The Nimiipuu made an agreement with Lewis and Clark to share peace and goodwill with white people. This solid relationship lasted for over seventy years until June 1876, when violence broke out against the wishes of Chief Joseph, leading to the famous Nimiipuu retreat.

LEWIS AND CLARK: A DOG INCIDENT

On their return journey in 1806, Lewis and Clark again stayed with the Nimiipuu, this time for an extended period as they waited for the snow to melt in the mountains. The persistently hungry Corps had developed a taste for dog meat. During their journey, the company had purchased many dogs from the Natives to eat. The Nimiipuu did not eat dog meat; they were repulsed by this feature of the Soyapo diet.

As Lewis ate a bowl of dog stew one evening, he reported that a young Nimiipuu threw a puppy at him "by way of derision for our eating dogs." Lewis caught the puppy, threw it back at the Nimiipuu man, hit him in the "breast and face," violently threatened him with his tomahawk, then "continued my repast on dog without further molestation."[18]

This incident involves many issues, explicit and implicit: race, power, diplomacy, the inevitability of conquest and oppression, and anger management, just to name a few. What we don't know about the confrontation is as important and interesting as what we do know. Why did Lewis do this? Was the behavior purposeful? Why did Lewis report this? Is this a confession, bold boasting, or a cultural difference? Does the act represent oppressive power, retaliation, or simply exhaustion? How is this related to teaching?

Meriwether Lewis' skirmish with the young Nimiipuu man reflects how teachers can feel when interacting with students. Many experienced educators will recognize Lewis' spontaneous rage. The dog incident caught Lewis off guard, made him feel subordinate, and challenged his authority. The unsettled nature of power dynamics between the white explorers and Native people can be helpful to teachers who reflect on the power aspects of their relationship with students.

STUDENT-TEACHER RELATIONSHIPS

The relationship between students and teachers is often discussed in glowing terms. But the relationship is complex, and at times contradictory. Teachers have something that students desire: a grade. Educational relationships are more complex than most interactions.

The relationship between the Nimiipuu and the white settlers was similarly fraught. The Nimiipuu were highly respected by white people, who in many cases desired to treat them fairly and with respect. However, the Natives had something that the whites desired: beautiful, productive land, with gold in it! Both Natives and whites strongly desired the land, creating an existential conflict between the two groups.

White farmers stole land along rivers, and ranchers used pasture land to graze livestock previously reserved for Nimiipuu horses and camas fields. Joseph summarized, "When I think of our condition my heart is heavy. I see men of my race treated as outlaws and driven from country to country, shot down like animals."[19]

Once the conflict began in 1877, Chief Joseph provided strong leadership and ethical decision-making, in the midst of an aggressive white invasion and takeover. Joseph summarized the sad situation, "I learned then that we were but few, while the white men were many, and that we could not hold our own with them. We were like deer. They were like grizzly bears."[20] Joseph remained dignified, intelligent, and steadfast throughout the transfer from Nimiipuu self-determination to white control of the region.

Joseph's actions were consistent with his statement: "I believe much trouble would be saved if we opened our hearts more."[21] Teaching is mysterious and challenging due to differences in values and customs. The white settlers lost sight of their moral and ethical values to pursue land, wealth, religious conversion, and gold. Students can lose sight of their values to pursue a diploma, or merely pass a class without learning.

Whites and Natives had different values in many areas: religion, culture, property rights, land, communication, relationships, and the appropriate meat to eat. The solution to these differences is civility, empathy, communication. Perhaps most importantly, respect.

A Standing Rock Sioux tribe member Vive Deloria Jr. reflected, "The foremost requirement in maintaining a society is that of mutual respect among its members. Lewis and Clark, from their comments in their journals, had little respect for the Indians or their institutions."[22] Several decades later, Joseph responded to this continuing disregard, "We ask to be recognized as men. We ask that the same law shall work alike on all men."[23]

How do teachers deal with the conflict inherent in teaching? Joseph and his people were treated miserably. Joseph faced enormous, existential duress throughout his entire adult life. Yet, he made the most out of a horrible situation. Joseph maintained hope, optimism, composure, and dignity even in the most difficult situation imaginable. Teachers would like students to dedicate effort to learning, and to treat their teachers and other students with respect. Students want to pass the course or achieve a certain grade. Sometimes, the interests of teachers and students are aligned, and sometimes they are not.

Given the potential divergence between students and teachers, teachers can provide a stable and productive learning environment, to the best of their ability. Lahtinen summarizes this belief: "To interact successfully with students the teachers need interpersonal skills that consist of the professional ability to work effectively with people, to treat them with respect as individuals and to help them develop their social potential."[24]

At times, there will be a polarization of power and authority. A skillful compromise can be employed to proactively maintain the productive environment and relationships. Even in difficult situations, teachers can think creatively, and do the best that they can. Joseph's true gift was diplomacy, in the face of the worst possible conditions.

Chief Joseph thought creatively about situations, resulting in solutions that did not compromise his principles, similar to Gandhi, as explored in chapter 9. Joseph's quick adaptation to rapidly changing situations allowed him to move forward through severe challenges. Joseph adopted his language and arguments to those that whites would accept. He argued that the land was his religion, knowing that whites would provide more respect to arguments based on religion. He also argued that the land contained the remains of his ancestors, knowing that his oppressors would have difficulty removing him from his ancestral home.

Joseph also confronted the deep and continuing dishonesty of the white settlers and US government: "Our fathers gave us many laws, which they had learned from their fathers. These laws were good. They told us to treat all men as they treated us; that we should never be the first to break a bargain; that it was a disgrace to tell a lie; that we should speak only the truth."[25]

Joseph explained the challenging emotional dynamics between Nimiipuu and white settlers: "since the white men came to Wallowa, we have been threatened and taunted by them and the treaty Nez Perce . . . [white friends] have always advised my people to bear these taunts without fighting. Our young men were quick tempered, and I have had great trouble in keeping them from doing rash things."[26]

Teaching and learning are challenging, both intellectually and interpersonally. Therefore, education can be emotional for both students and teachers. Mayes contends that to achieve classroom success, a teacher's emotional and cultural insights, tact, and "gentleness, honor, compassion, and psychological savvy are indispensable."[27] Teach like Joseph!

Recognition that teaching and learning are highly interactive and emotional gives teachers the knowledge to make good decisions and react to emotional challenges appropriately. When teachers realize that emotional interactions are based on a student's past experiences, greater understanding, empathy, and positivity result.

CONCLUSION

When Joseph was young, Nimiipuu children took part in a sacred vigil: the vision quest. Each child received his or her name by divine revelation. The child departed the security of the village alone with no weapons, no clothes, no food, and no water. After hunger and thirst set in, the child experienced an altered state of consciousness. While in this deprived state, the Nimiipuu child would learn from the Great Spirit a sacred song that represented their name.

Joseph took part in the vision quest, and while in a dream state, the Great Spirit revealed his name: Hin-mah-too-yah-lat-kekt, roughly translated as "Thunder Rising to Loftier Mountain Heights." For the Nimiipuu, removing themselves from daily life and listening to the Great Spirit resulted in powerful information. The sacred songs were considered unquestionable, since they came from within. Teachers can also gain from a similar, modified, practice. Often, the act of taking time to reflect on a teaching challenge can clarify the issue. Seeking solutions from within can often deliver the most appropriate way forward. Teach with dignity and consideration!

INTERSECTIONS

He [Chief Joseph] tried every kind of peaceful means to gain his ends. Like Gandhi, he [Chief Joseph] pursued a policy of noncooperation, and when this failed, he unwillingly sought recourse to arms.

—Biographer Helen Addison Howard.[28]

TEACHING SUMMARY: RELATE TO STUDENTS LIKE CHIEF JOSEPH

- Use a student's "sense of place" to start a conversation, and build a relationship.
- Praise students frequently and often.
- Be diplomatic.
- Think of ways to explain and teach in a manner that will be understood by students, who are different than the teacher.
- Always maintain dignity and respect for others, even in the face of challenge or difficulties to the extent possible.
- Never give up your principles.

NOTES

1. Quotefancy, "Chief Joseph."
2. Nerburn, "Chief Joseph."
3. Haines, *Nez Percés*, 194–195.
4. Haines, *Nez Percés*, 318.
5. Nerburn, "Chief Joseph," 147.
6. Joseph and Hare, "Indian Affairs," 416.
7. Howard, *Saga*, xxiii.
8. Lahtinen, "Pedagogical Interaction," 482.
9. Lahtinen, "Pedagogical Interaction," 485.
10. New Perspectives, "One Sky."
11. Lahtinen, "Pedagogical Interaction," 482.

12. Lahtinen, "Pedagogical Interaction," 482.
13. Lahtinen, "Pedagogical Interaction," 482.
14. Halfmoon, "Nez Perce Eyes."
15. Clark, "Watkuese," 177.
16. Halfmoon, "Nez Perce Eyes."
17. Journals of Lewis and Clark Expedition. Meriwether Lewis, Monday May 1, 1806.
18. Journals of Lewis and Clark Expedition. Meriwether Lewis, Monday May 5, 1806.
19. Joseph and Hare, "Indian Affairs," 432.
20. Joseph and Hare, "Indian Affairs," 432.
21. Joseph and Hare, "Indian Affairs," 415.
22. Josephy, "Indian Eyes," 13.
23. Joseph and Hare, "Indian Affairs," 432.
24. Lahtinen, "Pedagogical Interaction," 483.
25. Joseph and Hare, "Indian Affairs," 415.
26. Joseph and Hare, "Indian Affairs," 420.
27. Mayes, "Hero's Journey," 54.
28. Howard, *Saga*, xxiv.

REFERENCES

Clark, Ella E. "Watkuese and Lewis and Clark." *Western Folklore* 12, no. 3 (1953): 175–178. doi: 10.2307/1497520.

Haines, Francis. *The Nez Percés: Tribesmen of the Columbia Plateau*. Norman, OK: University of Oklahoma Press, 1955. doi: 10.2307/480530.

Halfmoon, Otis. "Lewis and Clark through Nez Perce Eyes." *Lewis and Clark Trail Heritage Foundation*. http://www.lewis-clark.org/article/984

Howard, Helen Addison. *Saga of Chief Joseph*. Caldwell, ID: Caxton Printers, 1941.

Joseph, Young, and William H. Hare. "An Indian's Views of Indian Affairs." *The North American Review* 128, no. 269 (1879): 412–433.

Josephy, Alvin M., ed. *Lewis and Clark through Indian Eyes*. New York: Vintage, 2007.

Journals of Lewis and Clark Expedition. Website. Accessed January 13, 2021. https://lewisandclarkjournals.unl.edu/

Lahtinen, Aino-Maija. "University Teachers' Views on the Distressing Elements of Pedagogical Interaction." *Scandinavian Journal of Educational Research* 52, no. 5 (2008): 481–493. doi: 10.1080/00313830802346363.

Mayes, Clifford. *The Archetypal Hero's Journey in Teaching and Learning: A Study in Jungian Pedagogy*. Madison, WI: Atwood, 2010.

Nerburn, Kent, ed. "Chief Joseph." In *The Wisdom of the Native Americans: Including the Soul of an Indian and Other Writings of Ohiyesa and the Great Speeches of Red Jacket, Chief Joseph, and Chief Seattle*, 147–188. Novato, CA: New World Library, 2010.

New Perspectives on the West. Episode Eight (1877-1914). "One Sky above Us." *PBS documentary series*, September 1996. Accessed January 1, 2021. https://www.pbs.org/weta/thewest/program/episodes/eight/thegift.htm

Quotefancy. "Chief Joseph Quotes." Accessed July 24, 2021. https://quotefancy.com/quote/1262486/Chief-Joseph-It-does-not-require-many-words-to-speak-the-truth

Chapter 8

Challenge and Support

Nelson Mandela

Figure 8.1   Nelson Mandela. *Source*: Wikimedia Commons. Library of the London School of Economics and Political Science—Nelson Mandela, 2000.

The greatest glory in living is not in falling, but in rising every time we fall.

—Nelson Mandela[1]

When people are determined they can overcome anything.

—Nelson Mandela[2]

CHAPTER SYNOPSIS

Nelson Mandela was a highly respected black South African leader. Apartheid, an oppressive white supremacist regime, caused Mandela to become a revolutionary freedom fighter. He was arrested and incarcerated for twenty-seven years, but later forgave his oppressors and worked together with his enemies to forge the inclusive new South African "Rainbow Nation." Mandela believed that the best way to influence others is by being a positive and respectful role model. The educational concept of challenge and support is presented, with examples drawn from Mandela's life and work.

Nelson Rolihlahla Mandela is considered to be the "father" of modern South Africa. Born in a small rural village in 1918 to the village chief, Mandela is known for leading a movement of freedom fighters to overthrow an authoritarian white supremacist government and replacing it with a liberal democracy. Mandela's given name was Rolihlahla, or "troublemaker." Perhaps this name was prophetic, given Mandela's lifetime work of disruption in the pursuit of positive change. Nelson's father died when he was nine years old. He was adopted by the leader of a neighboring village, Chief Jongintaba Dalindyebo, the acting regent of the Thembu people.

Mandela's interest in politics was sparked by listening to tribal elders at community meetings led by his guardian at the "Great Place," under three blue gum trees: "Everyone who wanted to speak did so. It was democracy in its purest form . . . the foundation of self-government was that all men were free to voice their opinions and equal in their value as citizens."[3]

Nelson's stepfather, the regent, had an important saying: "A leader, he said, is like a shepherd. He stays behind the flock, letting the most nimble go out ahead, whereupon the others follow, not realizing that all along they are being directed from behind."[4] This became Mandela's leadership style in the fight for freedom, and later as president of South Africa.

Mandela described his approach to management: "As a leader, I have always followed the principles I first saw demonstrated by the regent at the Great Place. I have always endeavored to listen to what each and every person in a discussion had to say before venturing my opinion. Oftentimes, my own opinion will simply represent a consensus of what I heard in the discussion."[5] After a childhood spent in the rural village, watching and learning from his stepfather, Mandela attended law school, then moved to Johannesburg, where he became active in anticolonial and African nationalist politics.

SOUTH AFRICA: A BRIEF HISTORY

People have lived in the region of South Africa for over 170,000 years. The Bantu people migrated to the region that is now South Africa about 1,500 years ago. Europeans arrived in South Africa in the fifteenth century, and began to settle the area in the early seventeenth century. The Europeans brought trade and cattle, enslaved people from other countries, and engaged in war with the indigenous people of the region.

British and Dutch settlers fought ferociously for ownership and control of South African land and resources. The conflict intensified after the discovery of diamonds in 1867 and gold in 1884. Economic control over these valuable resources led to increasing racial discrimination, segregation, and oppression. In 1948, the white supremacist National Party was elected to power. At the time, the white minority comprised only 20 percent of the population, but controlled the entire nation, including the majority black population.

Legal segregation became known as "apartheid," or "separateness" in Afrikaans, the language of Dutch settlers. Under this institutionalized system, whites enjoyed a high standard of living, and the black majority suffered enormous injustice, daily discrimination, and violent actions. Violence was used to crack down on black dissent and opposition to the white government.

LEADERSHIP UNDER OPPRESSION

At the time of National Party rule, Nelson Mandela was a young leader of the African National Congress (ANC), a political organization founded to bring all Africans together and defend their rights and freedoms. Racial segregation and oppression led Mandela to lead mass protests and civil disobedience campaigns in the attempt to end the racist regime. Mandela was motivated to try to stop the crushing racial discrimination: "I was prepared to use whatever means to speed up the erasure of human prejudice and the end of chauvinistic and violent nationalism."[6]

In 1961, Mandela founded Umkhonto we Sizwe (the Spear of the Nation), the military branch of the ANC: "For me, nonviolence was not a moral principle but a strategy; there is no moral goodness in using an ineffective weapon."[7] He was actively involved in planning attacks against the white government infrastructure until his arrest in 1962.

Mandela was put on trial, where he explained his actions to the court: "I have fought against white domination and I have fought against black domination. I have cherished the idea of a democratic and a free society in which all persons live together in harmony and with equal opportunity. It is an ideal which I hope to live for and to achieve. But, my Lord, if need be, it is an ideal for which I am prepared to die."[8]

After a long trial, Mandela was sentenced to life imprisonment in 1964. He spent seventeen years in the notoriously harsh prison on Robben Island, about four miles off the coast of Cape Town. People throughout the world observed the horrors of apartheid, and the detention of South African black leaders. During his incarceration, Mandela became the world's most famous prisoner, and an icon for standing up for freedom in South Africa. After twenty-seven years in prison, Mandela was released on February 11, 1990.

Mandela's experience in prison caused a reevaluation of his goals, methods, and leadership strategies. Biographer John Carlin states that prior to his prison sentence, Mandela acknowledged that prison had a large influence on him: "He went in angry, convinced the only way of achieving his people's freedom was by force of arms."[9] While in jail, Mandela spent a great deal of time observing human behavior of black prisoners, white prison guards, and the interaction between the two groups.

Carlin explained, "He learnt that succumbing to the vengeful passions brought fleeting joys at the cost of lasting benefits," reflecting Gandhi's nonviolent approach to social change (chapter 9). Years of reflection in prison resulted in Mandela's mature political strategy: "he learnt through studying the jailors closely, that black and white people had far more in common, at bottom, than they had points of difference; he learnt that forgiveness and generosity and, above all, respect were weapons of political persuasion as powerful as any gun."[10]

Forgiveness and generosity are at the core of Mandela. These traits resulted in Mandela becoming a political leader of unconventionally high levels of politeness and respect for others. After release from prison, Mandela returned to politics, and was elected to be the first black president of South Africa in April 1994. As president, Mandela focused on reconciliation between all ethnic groups. Mandela's legacy includes the replacement of apartheid and oppression with the rule of law, freedom of speech, free and fair elections, and democracy.

With Archbishop Desmond Tutu, he organized the Truth and Reconciliation Committee which assisted in moving forward, past the crimes and oppression committed by the previous government under apartheid. After a five-year term as president, Mandela retired from politics, and dedicated himself to social causes including the promotion of children and HIV-AIDS.

IMPERFECT HERO

Like all heroes, Mandela's greatness is imperfect. Mandela received criticism throughout his life as a freedom fighter, prisoner, elected politician, and social activist. Many critics argue that his communist ties and beliefs are problematic. Others condemn his use of violence and refer to Mandela as a terrorist. Mandela was open and honest about all of his limitations.

Leaders who do great things become the target of high expectations, criticism, and blame. Mandela's long list of negative assessments shows that his success as a revolutionary led to the belief that Mandela could and should solve all political, social, and economic problems. This form of criticism is commonly leveled against national leaders. Unfortunately, it is also common for teachers, the leaders of students.

Many students expect perfection from their teachers. Teachers, like politicians, are imperfect. Mandela shared, "Only armchair politicians are immune from committing mistakes. Errors are inherent in political action. Those who are in the centre of political struggles, who have to deal with practical and pressing problems, are afforded little time for reflection and no precedents to guide them and are bound to slip up many times."[11] This idea provides sustenance to battle-weary teachers and those who have erred. Don't let mistakes paralyze you into inaction or depression; your students need you to stay strong. Teach like Mandela by moving forward!

MOTIVATION

Teachers who reflect on Mandela's life experiences can gain important inspiration. Many teachers believe that their impact on students outweighs personal ambitions. Educators are often willing to give up financial reward and career success to help students succeed. Mandela stated, "What counts in life is not the mere fact that we have lived. It is what difference we have made to the lives of others that will determine the significance of the life we lead."[12]

Mandela provides motivation for teachers to help others learn, grow, and prosper: "There can be no greater gift than that of giving one's time and energy to help others without expecting anything in return."[13] Teachers who focus on the details of helping others can improve the world. When teachers are bombarded with the business of preparing for class, grading, and interpersonal interactions, they can gain perspective by recalling Mandela's wisdom: in times of stress or duress, focus on helping others.

COOPERATION AND TEAMWORK

Mandela placed great importance on community as a way of achieving great things in the world: "To be free is not merely to cast off one's chains, but to live in a way that respects and enhances the freedom of others."[14] Like Martin Luther King, Jr. (chapter 11), Mandela emphasized that we must seek to eliminate injustice wherever it exists: "While poverty persists, there is no true freedom."[15] Educators have a unique position to teach students about injustice and poverty. Sharing the world's tainted history and desire to make our lives better can have a large and lasting effect on student views and desire to help others.

Mandela's hallmark was his willingness to work with, compromise, and forgive his enemies. This is a unique characteristic, rare among humans and political leaders. Teachers who minimize blame, resentments, and strife will move the world forward at a faster rate using their precious energy in the pursuit of goodness, rather than toward unproductive activities.

Mandela's sense of forgiveness was not necessarily religious or spiritual. Rather, it was simply pragmatic: he desired to improve the world, and knew that progress requires working with people who have different viewpoints, opinions, and actions. Had Mandela not worked with the white supremacist leaders of apartheid, change would not have occurred. Mandela shared some straightforward advice about how to be a true leader: "To make peace with an enemy, one must work with that enemy, and that enemy becomes one's partner."[16]

Forgiveness is a simple, powerful idea for educators. In classroom situations, a student may appear to be an "enemy." Not a political or military enemy, but an individual who opposes following the teacher's rules, instructions, or ideas. Difficult students will often respond more positively to encouraging support rather than displays of power or authoritarian attempts to control a challenging student. Kindness is more likely to resolve challenges than domination.

The way forward is extravagant positivity and praise, proactively forgiving students for any past, current, or future transgressions. Mandela explained: "People are human beings, produced by the society in which they live. You encourage people by seeing the good in them."[17] Mandela's life and work emphasized working well with others: "If you are humble, you are no threat to anybody. Some behave in a way that dominates others. That's a mistake."[18]

Mandela's respect for others shines through: "If you want the cooperation of humans around you, you must make them feel they are important—and you do that by being genuine and humble. You know that other people have qualities that may be better than your own. Let them express them."[19] Teachers can be quick to evaluate opposing views from students as incorrect. Mandela suggests an open-minded approach to classroom dialogue and divergent opinions. Teachers can enhance student learning by striving to find a piece of the truth in all student views, and gently discuss strengths and weaknesses of stated opinions.

Mandela spoke eloquently about relationships: "People respond in accordance to how you relate to them. If you approach them on the basis of violence, that's how they'll react. But if you say we want peace, we want stability, we can then do a lot of things that will contribute towards the progress of our society."[20] This quote ties individual behavior with societal outcomes: teachers have the unique and solemn responsibility of influencing student thoughts, minds, and futures.

CROSS-FERTILIZATION

Mandela was a strong promoter of working with a diverse group of people to achieve the most productive ideas: "I like friends who have independent minds because they tend to make you see problems from all angles."[21] Teachers can benefit from new and different ideas.

The concept of cross-fertilization comes from biology, where it refers to reproduction arising from different parents. In education, the term refers to a productive interchange of different ideas, cultures, or categories. When new ideas are imported and blended with old notions, the product is often greater than the sum of the parts. Economists call this "complementarity," and in business this idea is called, "synergy."

Gains are largest when differences are largest: complementary ideas are more valuable and relevant when they come from divergent sources. Ideas that are most productive are often from unexpected sources. Educators who read widely, interact with people who are different from themselves, and learn new things can enhance student learning by bringing innovative ideas to the classroom.

Professional meetings and workshops for educators can provide new insights, often from surprising sources. Mandela's prison experience shows that interaction with others can lead to greater understanding, higher levels of effectiveness, and positive outcomes. Often, fear of people or students who differ from ourselves is a result of a lack of experience.

Interaction and shared experience can be enormously productive: people who know each other are more likely to be able to work together with understanding and cooperation. Difficulties are more likely to be worked out when people have built a relationship before the challenge arises. Fear of others who are different from ourselves is quickly replaced with mutual respect, empathy, and understanding. The transition from fear to friendship is often immediate, as it is great fun to connect with and learn from new people.

CHALLENGE AND SUPPORT

Psychology Professor Nevitt Sanford created the "challenge and support" model of student development.[22] The idea is that student growth occurs when the correct balance is found between challenge and support. The model suggests that too much challenge leads to unproductive stress, and too much support leads to disengagement and low levels of effort. Both situations lead to lower levels of student learning. Effective teachers can push student intellectual development (challenge) and work to help students meet these challenges (support).

Mandela on *challenge*: "The challenge for each one of you is to take up the ideals of tolerance and respect for others and put them to practical use in your schools, your communities, and throughout our lives."[23] Mandela on *support*: "There can be no greater gift than that of giving one's time and energy to helping others without expecting anything in return."[24]

Reflecting on challenge and support can enhance a teacher's ability to maximize student learning outcomes. This can be accomplished by brainstorming as many ideas as possible that could balance challenge and support. This activity can be done as an individual, or with others. Ideas from non-teachers can be most insightful and effective, due to cross-fertilization of ideas. Once a list of possible teaching strategies is complete, identify the most productive and pragmatic ideas, and implement them as soon as possible. Differences in approach and style can bring great synergies.

Academic coaching, a pedagogical style where the teacher's role is less like a formal instructor and more like a coach, provides a proven method to match the level of challenge and support.[25] A coaching approach to teaching results in a proactive relationship between teachers and students, responsive to student learning outcomes and committed to learning success.

The flipped classroom has become a common educational practice, where lectures are moved outside of class time, and class is used for inquiry-based learning. The flipped classroom can be a good way to implement the challenge and support model by increasing and personalizing student-teacher interaction.[26] The flipped classroom often includes team-based assignments, quizzes, and exams, where students take responsibility for their own learning.

The flipped pedagogy follows Mandela's leadership strategies of building respectful relationships with others, even those who are challenging or difficult. Rather than using class time for formal lectures or classroom presentations, it is used for collaborations with students and promoting learning. The flipped classroom provides the ability for a teacher to share ideas, promote positivity about the course material, the students, teamwork, and life itself. A teacher can implement Mandela's principles of treating others well and providing a positive approach and a nurturing learning environment.

CONCLUSION

Nelson Mandela's life provides fertile ground for professional growth. Mandela provides a uniquely rich and generous model for teachers: "There is no passion to be found playing small—in settling for a life that is less than the one you are capable of living."[27] When teaching, Mandela suggests: "A good head and a good heart are always a formidable combination."[28] During difficult times, he reminds us of his own life experience: "After climbing a great hill. One only finds that there are many more hills to climb."[29]

Crucially, Mandela also prescribed perseverance in the face of difficulty: "Do not judge me by my successes, judge me by how many times I fell down and got back up again."[30] Mandela emphasized that mistakes and problems are part of professional growth and development: "It is in the character of growth that we should learn from both pleasant and unpleasant experiences."[31] What a thrill to recognize that all teaching experiences can improve teacher effectiveness, and can be used to improve the lives of students.

INTERSECTIONS

What I will remember most about Mr. Mandela is that he was a man whose heart, soul and spirit could not be contained or restrained by racial and economic injustices, metal bars or the burden of hate and revenge. He taught us forgiveness on a grand scale.

—Muhammad Ali[32]

He inspired others to reach for what appeared to be impossible and moved them to break through the barriers that held them hostage mentally, physically, socially and economically. He made us realize, we are our brother's keeper and that our brothers come in all colors.

—Muhammad Ali[33]

Muhammad Ali was not just my hero, but the hero of millions of young, black South Africans because he brought dignity to boxing. I respected

Ali's decision not to go to Vietnam. He made a principled statement about why such a war was unjust and incorrect and I admired him for refusing to go. . . . He was an inspiration to me, even in prison, because I thought of his courage and his commitment to his sport.

—Nelson Mandela[34]

For a young lady of that nature to take a stand is something unique. Her life was one on which young people could model their own lives and that is what was striking about the life of Anne Frank.

—Nelson Mandela[35]

TEACHING SUMMARY: CHALLENGE AND SUPPORT LIKE NELSON MANDELA

- Teach from behind: allow the most capable students to show the way, then support and direct from behind. Listen carefully to every student, then speak. Other people have great qualities; let them express them, and integrate their ideas into your teaching.
- Forgive students, colleagues, and administrators, including those who have done wrong to you. Forgiveness is Mandela's greatest legacy, and most powerful weapon: forgiveness liberates the soul, and removes fear.
- Respect all individuals, even if you disagree with them. Especially rivals and enemies.
- Stand up against all injustice. Maintain awareness of oppression. Respect and enhance the freedom of others. While poverty exits, there is no true freedom.
- In times of stress or duress, help others.
- Recall that progress requires working with people with different viewpoints and opinions.
- Enhance student learning outcomes by seeking the correct balance between challenge and support for effective student development.
- Try "Academic Coaching" or a "Flipped Classroom" to follow Mandela's leadership style with a focus on interactions and relationships between teachers and students.

NOTES

1. Mandela, Address at 1998 Clinton reception.
2. Mandela, *By Himself*, 71.
3. Mandela, *Long Walk*, 21.
4. Mandela, *Long Walk*, 22.

5. Mandela, *Long Walk*, 22.
6. Mandela, *Long Walk*, 121.
7. Mandela, *Long Walk*, 158.
8. Mandela, "Prepared to Die."
9. Carlin, *Legacy*.
10. Carlin, *Legacy*.
11. Mandela, *By Himself*, 146.
12. Mandela, "On Life."
13. Mandela, "Address at Harlow Butler Ceremony."
14. Mandela, *Long Walk*, 624.
15. Mandela, "Poverty."
16. Mandela, *Long Walk*, 612.
17. Mandela, *By Himself*, 162.
18. Winfrey, *Oprah Talks*.
19. Winfrey, *Oprah Talks*.
20. O'Connell, *Nelson Mandela?*
21. Mandela, *By Himself*, 99.
22. Sanford, *American College*.
23. Mandela, *By Himself*, 390.
24. Mandela, *Notes*, 146.
25. Barkley, *Academic Coaching*, 76.
26. Barkley, *Flipping*, 240.
27. BrainyQuote, "Nelson Mandela."
28. Blackwell and Hobday. *Nelson Mandela.*
29. BrainyQuote, "Nelson Mandela."
30. McKenna, "15 Quotes."
31. Mandela, *Foreign Correspondents*.
32. Schreiner, *Boxing Great*.
33. LoGiurato, *Statement*.
34. Bingham, *Thirty Year*.
35. Mandela, *By Himself*, 72.

REFERENCES

Barkley, Andrew. "Academic Coaching for Enhanced Learning." *NACTA Journal* 55, no. 1 (March 2011): 76–81.

Barkley, Andrew. "Flipping the College Classroom for Enhanced Student Learning." *NACTA Journal* 59, no. 1 (September 2015): 240–244.

Bingham, Howard. *Muhammad Ali–A Thirty-year Journey*, New York: Simon & Schuster, 1993.

Blackwell, Geoff, and Ruth Hobday. *I Know This to Be True: Nelson Mandela.* San Francisco, CA: Chronicle Books, 2020.

BrainyQuote. "Nelson Mandela Quotes." Accessed June 15, 2021. https://www.brainyquote.com/quotes/nelson_mandela_391070

Carlin, John. "Nelson Mandela's Legacy," *The Cairo Review of Social Affairs*, Summer 2011. Accessed May 26, 2021. https://www.thecairoreview.com/essays/ nelson-mandelas-legacy/

LoGiurato, Brett. "Muhammad Ali's Statement on Nelson Mandela's Death Is Beautiful," *Insider*, December 5, 2013. Accessed June 25, 2021. https://www.businessinsider.com/muhammad-ali-statement-nelson-mandela-death-dead-2013-12

Mandela, Nelson. Address by Nelson Mandela at the acknowledgement ceremony of FCB Harlow Butler, Nelson Mandela Foundation, Johannesburg, South Africa, February 27, 2004. Accessed June 10, 2021. http://www.mandela.gov.za/mandela _speeches/2004/040227_butler.htm

Mandela, Nelson. Address by Nelson Mandela at reception hosted by President Clinton White House. Washington, DC. September 22, 1998. Accessed June 15, 2021. http://db.nelsonmandela.org/speeches/pub_view.asp?pg=item&ItemID =NMS633&txtstr=greatest%20glory

Mandela, Nelson. Foreign Correspondents' Association Annual Dinner, Johannesburg, South Africa, November 21, 1997. Accessed June 27, 2021. https://www.nelson-mandela.org/uploads/files/Nelson_Mandela_By_Himself_Publicity_Guidelines.pdf

Mandela, Nelson. "I am Prepared to Die: Nelson Mandela's Statement from the Dock at the Opening of the Defence Case in the Rivonia Trial," April 20, 1964. *Nelson Mandela Centre of Memory. Nelson Mandela Foundation.* Accessed May 27, 2021. http://db.nelsonmandela.org/speeches/pub_view.asp?pg=item&ItemID=NMS010

Mandela, Nelson. *Long Walk to Freedom: The Autobiography of Nelson Mandela.* New York: Little, Brown, and Company, 1994.

Mandela, Nelson. *Nelson Mandela by Himself: The Authorised Book of Quotations.* Johannesburg, South Africa: Macmillan; 1st Edition, 2013.

Mandela, Nelson. "Nelson Mandela on Life," 90th Birthday celebration of Walter Sisulu, Walter Sisulu Hall, Randburg, Johannesburg, South Africa. May 18, 2002. Accessed June 10, 2021. http://db.nelsonmandela.org/speeches/pub_view.asp?pg =item&ItemID=NMS708&txtstr=Walter

Mandela, Nelson. *Notes to the Future: Words of Wisdom*, New York: Simon & Schuster, 2012.

Mandela, Nelson. Speech for the "Make Poverty History" campaign. Trafalgar Square, London. February 3, 2005. Accessed June 10, 2021. http://news.bbc.co.uk /2/hi/uk_news/politics/4232603.stm

McKenna, Amy. "15 Nelson Mandela Quotes." *Britannica Encyclopedia.* Accessed June 15, 2021. https://www.britannica.com/list/nelson-mandela-quotes

O'Connell, Caitlin. "Who Is Nelson Mandela? A Reader's Digest Exclusive Interview," *Reader's Digest*, updated June 28, 2017. Accessed June 24, 2021. https://www.rd .com/list/who-is-nelson-mandela-a-readers-digest-exclusive-interview/

Sanford, N. *The American College.* New York: Wiley, 1962.

Schreiner, Bruce. "Boxing Great Muhammad Ali pays tribute to Mandela," *AP News*, December 5, 2013. Accessed June 25, 2021. https://apnews.com/article/e04189e 395b444dcb584b45554790d8e

Winfrey, Oprah. "Oprah Talks to Nelson Mandela," *O, The Oprah Magazine,* April 2001. Accessed June 24, 2022. https://www.oprah.com/world/oprah-interviews -nelson-mandela/all#ixzz6ykE3Qh91

Chapter 9

Power from Oppression

Mahatma Gandhi

Figure 9.1   Mahatma Gandhi. *Source*: Wikimedia Commons. Elliott & Fry.

You must be the change you wish to see in the world.
                                    —Mahatma Gandhi[1]

Live as if you were to die tomorrow; learn as if you were to live forever.
                                    —Mahatma Gandhi[2]

CHAPTER SYNOPSIS

Gandhi fought to end injustice and oppression, and he changed the way we fight for freedom and against injustice. Gandhi's philosophy of nonviolence inspired Martin Luther King, Jr. to advance civil rights in the United States. Gandhi's personal convictions, developed over a lifetime of public service, provide a powerful strategy for successful teaching using a deep sense of truth to avoid and resolve conflict. Gandhi demonstrated the importance for teachers to model what they desire their students to be.

Indian politician Mahatma Gandhi (1869–1948) developed a unique approach to fighting injustice. He named his method of nonviolent resistance *Satyagraha*, meaning "truth force," or "soul force." *Satyagraha* refers to "holding fast to truth," "adherence to truth," "insistence on truth," and "reliance on truth."[3] Gandhi changed the world by shifting the focus of conflict from persons to principles. Without resorting to violence, Gandhi led the successful fight to end the British colonization of India.

Gandhi was designated the "Father of India" for his leadership role in the independence movement. His birthday is celebrated as a national holiday in India to commemorate his exceptional accomplishments. Gandhi was a religious person and spiritual leader. He strongly advocated for the poor and dispossessed and was a model of ethical living. Gandhi exhibited the rare ability to fuse personal beliefs with public actions. There was no distinction between Gandhi's religious beliefs and his political strategies. He said, "My life is my message."[4]

Gandhi was not an ideal role model. He made mistakes and experienced failure throughout his life. Gandhi was completely open about his shortcomings: he wrote about them, publicly acknowledged them, and atoned for them. His openness was so complete as to be disarming and threatening to rivals.

Gandhi developed his ideas, philosophies, and approaches throughout his life of public service. Gandhi's efforts led to great achievements during his life, and a legacy of enduring and universal ideas that remain after his death. The "truth force" of *satyagraha* used to fight oppression in India, was adopted by other leaders fighting injustice, including Martin Luther King Jr. in the United States, Lech Walesa in Poland, and Vaclav Havel in Czechoslovakia.

Gandhi's legacy is enormous and continuing. He is distinguished not only for his efforts to bring independence to India but also for his leadership in the elimination of the untouchable caste, promotion of religious harmony, and development of environmental sustainability. Mohandas Karamchand Gandhi was born in 1869 in a small town in western India. After a short childhood, he married at age thirteen to Kasturba, aged fourteen. The arranged marriage was in line with the cultural practices in India at that time.

In 1888, Gandhi moved to London for Law School, graduating in 1891. After graduation, he spent a short time in India before Gandhi and Kasturba moved to South Africa to open a law practice. Gandhi's life of protest and reform began in Durban, after experiencing racist behavior directed at him. He had been taunted, disrespected, and thrown off of a train for sitting in the first-class rail car, reserved for whites.

Gandhi spent twenty-one years in South Africa, a British colony at the time, fighting racial injustice and protecting the rights of Indians who lived there. During this time, he began to formulate his views on race, oppression, and colonialism. In 1915, at age forty-six, he returned to a hero's welcome in India for his successful battle against unethical and racist British laws in South Africa. At this time, the movement for Indian independence from Britain was taking hold.

Gandhi became a political leader, but his reputation took on spiritual attributes, leading to new names for Gandhi. The suffix "ji" was added to his name to indicate respect: Gandhiji. The honorific title "Mahatma," or "Great Soul" was given to him to demonstrate love and respect. Gandhi's life was an attempt to live according to religious values. The application of eternal truths to daily life is Gandhi's continuing legacy. Biographer Ramachandra Guha concluded that, "Beyond *satyagraha* . . . the practice of, and the largely successful quest for, truth may in fact be Gandhi's most remarkable achievement."[5]

Upon his return to India, Gandhi's efforts evolved from combating unethical laws to fighting for *Swaraj*, or complete national independence for India. Gandhi spent the rest of his life on his dream of freedom from the oppression of colonial rule. Louis Fischer, biographer and friend of Gandhi stated: "The British were masters in somebody else's house. Their very presence was a humiliation. . . . Subjection breeds a desire for liberation. Here imperialism digs its own grave—and there can be no good colonizers."[6]

Gandhi's contribution was to take on the power, might, and long history of the British Empire, without the use of guns or violence. Gandhi's disregard for laws that he considered to be immoral and unethical resulted in a great deal of time in jail. To draw attention to his social and political intentions, Gandhi practiced fasting, or refraining from food. Gandhi succeeded with nonviolence, "First they ignore you, then they laugh at you, then they fight you, then you win."[7]

His unique approach brought Gandhi iconic status. Gandhi was gifted at drawing positive attention to his causes through his lifestyle, clothing, and appearance. He dressed in a *Dhoti*, the traditional clothing of the poor in

India. Gandhi lived simply, renounced material possessions, and took a vow of celibacy. These acts of renunciation allowed Gandhi to focus more deeply and directly on his life's work: improving the human condition through *satyagraha*, the truth force.

TRUTH FORCE

In his early work to fight oppression and injustice, Gandhi found that violence harms the perpetrator as well as the victim. In response, Gandhi developed the idea of *satyagraha*. Truth force was based on nonviolent action to promote good in the world, with truth broadly defined to encompass: (1) truth in speech, (2) what is real, and (3) doing good.[8]

The origins of Gandhi's belief in nonviolence are ancient. The Jain religion, commonly practiced in Gandhi's hometown, is a Hindu reform church that subscribes to *ahisma*, the prohibition of killing any living creature. Gandhi's ethical philosophy was also influenced by the American Henry David Thoreau, who believed that doing what was right involved civil disobedience to change immoral or unjust laws. Gandhi stated, "I object to violence because when it appears to do good, the good is only temporary; the evil it does is permanent."[9]

During his stay in South Africa, Gandhi corresponded with author Leo Tolstoy. Tolstoy, a Christian, suggested "Whenever you are confronted with an opponent, conquer him with love."[10] Tolstoy strived to connect this religious belief with everyday actions, behavior, and thoughts. These ideals influenced Gandhi's ideas on nonviolence and social change.

Gandhi's idea of truth force was also based on his reading of the Christian Bible, including Jesus' teaching to "love your enemies and pray for those who persecute you."[11] Gandhi was strongly influenced by the Sermon on the Mount's emphasis on providing aid to the least among us, and Jesus' advice in the Book of Matthew to "turn the other cheek." Gandhi prescribed courageously taking the high moral ground: "An eye for eye only ends up making the whole world blind."[12]

In this sense, *satyagraha* is compatible with Christianity, and captures the "soul force" of all major religions: The Golden Rule of treating others the way that you want to be treated. Gandhi's main source of inspiration and comfort was the sacred Hindu book, the *Bhagavad Gita*, which suggests that individuals have the right to perform duties, but are not entitled to the results, or outcomes, of their actions.

Gandhi insisted, "It's the action, not the fruit of the action, that's important. You have to do the right thing. It may not be in your power, may not be in your time, that there'll be any fruit. But that doesn't mean you stop doing the right thing. You may never know what results come from your action. But if you do nothing, there will be no result."[13]

Gandhi argued that British rule in India was only possible with the cooperation of Indians, and if Indians did not cooperate, the British would be forced to give up power and authority. Gandhi's civil disobedience and application of *satyagraha* drew imprisonment for Gandhi, and in many cases, violence against unarmed, nonviolent protesters.

As the British tightened their control of Indians through expansion of strict policies and violence, Gandhi strengthened his resolve through enhancement of his protest movement. Gandhi's approach is "process oriented" instead of "results oriented." Gandhi emphasized action: "The future depends on what you do today."[14] This approach is counter to the fast-paced modern life of the Western world. The British were threatened by Gandhi's moral argument. Nonviolence demands courage, since nonviolent adherents neither ignore injustice, nor walk away from the threat of being attacked. Gandhi said, "I am prepared to die, but there is no cause for which I am prepared to kill."[15]

In the end, Gandhi's *satyagraha* persuaded the British to quit India, an act that seemed completely impossible before Gandhi's leadership. After Indian independence, the British continued to withdraw from colonies throughout the world, until the Empire was dissolved. The most powerful global empire fell due to Gandhi's perseverance.

SATYAGRAHA FOR TEACHERS

Gandhi believed that conflict could be productive. He believed that all individuals know only a part of the whole truth, and each of us could expand our view through fighting with others. Much can be gained by learning how others view the world and incorporating opposing views into our own perspective. Gandhi developed *satyagraha* to show the world a new way of fighting, one that focuses on the way that we fight, rather than what we are fighting about. Gandhi's approach to fighting can enhance teaching and learning in deep and important ways.[16]

In what follows, the Gandhian view of conflict is developed with the knowledge of religion scholar and conflict resolution expert Mark Juergensmeyer and reporter and writer Eric Weiner. Gandhi's methodology for conflict can be applied to battles of any size: a simple spat, a family argument, a political debate, or armed conflict. For teachers, this could be an argument with a student, a feud with colleagues over pedagogy, or a battle with an administrator over institutional policy. Gandhi's main contribution is to find a win-win solution by creatively seeking the truth about the conflict and the principles underlying the disagreement.

Suppose that a teacher, Mr. Johnson, is struggling with a student, Claire, in the attempt to inspire greater presence, interest, and effort in a class activity. Mr. Johnson knows from many years of experience that the class material is likely to be useful to the student later in her career and life. Claire is not convinced, believing that the content is too abstract and removed from her current and future lifestyle to matter.

This divergence has existed throughout the term, but has recently manifested itself in a battle over a challenging assignment. Claire has made it known to her classmates and instructor that the assignment is simultaneously "irrelevant" and "too difficult." Mr. Johnson feels the sting of being publicly rebuked over an assignment that has for several years been a productive and effective pedagogical activity for students enrolled in the course. Claire has made her objections public, sewing doubt in her classmates' view of the course and Mr. Johnson's teaching ability.

Gandhi suggests that the first possible solution to such a standoff is "forced victory." Mr. Johnson could insist that the assignment be completed, with no exceptions. The penalty for late work could be punitive; the grading strict and retaliatory. These measures might cause Claire to do the assignment, solving the immediate battle, but likely exacerbate the underlying conflict. Claire's negative opinions about the subject matter would probably be reinforced by harsh tactics; her relationship with Mr. Johnson could be compromised further. As Jurgensmeyer notes, "The loser resents being bludgeoned into submission."[17]

Claire has some ability to win a "forced victory," too. She could recruit a group of students to boycott the assignment; involve her parents in a public protest of Mr. Johnson; disrupt class with nonstop questions; or worse. Gandhi suggested that the forced victory approach results in the undesirable outcome of an uneasy equilibrium and smoldering emotions.

A second means of dealing with the conflict is that of "accommodation," or yielding to the interests of the opponent. Mr. Johnson could make the assignment shorter, easier, or optional. In this case, students could put as much or as little effort into the assignment as they wished. The grade could be based solely on turning in the assignment, regardless of quality. Like forced victory, accommodation is not a desirable outcome. In this case, Mr. Johnson compromises the integrity of the learning process. Gandhi described this situation, "I cannot conceive of a greater loss than the loss of one's self-respect."[18]

Not only does Claire miss out on learning important concepts, but the rest of the class could be negatively affected by the truce. Claire could yield to Mr. Johnson by buckling down and agreeing to complete the assignment without complaint. But she is likely to harbor feelings of doing meaningless work on unimportant topics. Giving either victory or accommodation to the opponent may temporarily ease the frustrating situation, but is in Gandhi's opinion, a dishonest, "unclean" solution. Accommodation by Mr. Johnson causes him to feel dejected and incompetent. Accommodation by Claire perpetuates her negative views of the course material.

A third solution is "compromise." Each side gives something to the other. This solution sounds promising. Gandhi, however, argued that this solution is also fraught. Suppose Mr. Johnson offered Claire extra credit for completing the assignment, or offered her a chance to receive credit for an alternative assignment.

Suppose Claire offers to demonstrate kindness and civility in class if Mr. Johnson provides a way to receive credit without doing the assignment. These political deals may provide benefits to both parties. Gandhi emphasizes, however, that such a compromise solution also results in losses to both parties. Once again, Claire loses the knowledge that the assignment would provide, and Mr. Johnson loses his faith in providing a positive, engaging, and meaningful learning environment.

Another possible way of dealing with this issue is an "appeal" to authority, arbitration, or the rules. Claire could file a grievance against Mr. Johnson with the school administration. Mr. Johnson could demand a meeting with Claire's parents (if she is in K–12), or set up a meeting with a college administrator and Claire (is she is in higher education). This type of arbitration is almost always costly in terms of time, energy, and emotional duress.

Worse yet, the decider, or authority, in this case would make a determination that favored either Mr. Johnson or Claire. This solution is often a costly process that leads to the same outcomes as forced victory or compromise, with the same unresolved issues.

Gandhi proposes a completely different type of solution. *Satyagraha* requires rivals to completely rethink their adversary: "An opponent is not always bad simply because he opposes."[19] Maybe Gandhi is correct that Mr. Johnson and Claire each have a portion of the truth, but not all of the truth. If each of them could devote time to reflection and analysis, they might find some common ground, at a level deeper than the initial misunderstanding.

A Gandhian solution is one where both sides receive something that they didn't know they wanted. Perhaps Mr. Johnson has a need to feel that he is a competent, caring teacher, and Claire's challenge caused him to feel inadequate. Perhaps Claire felt that course material did not value her career interests, her life choices, or her strengths and abilities. Is there a way forward that resolves these underlying issues and emotions?

Gandhi suggests that violence is the result of a lack of creativity. Could a creative solution be found that causes both Mr. Johnson and Claire to drop the conflict, and move forward together toward a cooperative and productive relationship? What would happen if Mr. Johnson took time to talk to Claire about her interests, goals, and life experiences? Could the challenging assignment be directed toward Claire's values, experiences, and situation? Would this affirm Claire's need to matter?

If the course assignment were framed in a way that made it relevant, timely, and applicable to Claire, she is more likely to become excited about the course content. If Claire were to demonstrate enthusiasm, or even a lack of hostility, Mr. Johnson could meet his needs of feeling like he cared about his students by providing them with tools that would help them in the future. In this case, the pedagogical change was relatively small. The assignment remained the same; the motivation for the work was made more directly appropriate to Claire.

This is the power of Gandhi's way of looking at the world: a change in viewpoint resulted in large benefits to both parties. One can imagine Mr. Johnson's elation from resolving a challenging interpersonal conflict. He would also be overjoyed with the ability to help Claire. Claire might be exhilarated to have made a difference; to be noticed; to have had a positive impact; and most importantly, to create a better future for herself and her classmates. Gandhi suggests that we "strive to see not only the best in people, but their latent goodness, too."[20]

Gandhi's approach is effective, but requires effort. Teachers could ignore classroom difficulties, due to fatigue, indifference, or a lack of perceptiveness. Gandhi does not recommend this, as the suppressed emotions can distort teacher and student actions. After all, he suggests that, "You may never know what results come from your action, but if you do nothing, there will be no result."[21]

Suppression is an unclean, dishonest way of dealing with challenges. Instead, Gandhi proposes that teachers: (1) recognize an injustice and confront it, (2) battle creatively and clearly, and (3) above all, do not resort to violence. Here, the term "violence" can be broadly defined to include every action that causes harm to another individual, including emotional or mental anguish. The result may not be what the teacher was hoping for, but it could be even better.

The practice of "truth force" in the classroom changes the way we think about process and results. The use of violent means to seek a peaceful end is contradictory. And, it is often ineffective. A nation of people that uses violence to overthrow an oppressive regime is likely to fail. Nelson Mandela recognized this through reflection during his incarceration (chapter 8).

Juergensmeyer summarizes Gandhi's view: "Actions are habit forming. If you use coercion once, you increase the likelihood that you will use it again, and with every coercive act you build up a store of ill will in your opponent that decreases the possibility of a genuine resolution."[22] Teachers can usefully design methods to match their principles. The reason is not only for consistency and correctness; the means not only directly affect the result, but the means become a major part of the result.

A coercive solution results in harm to both parties. Teachers get out of a challenging situation is what they put into it. A creative solution that causes both teachers and students to be enthusiastic is not likely to come from thinking poorly about the opponent. Teachers who think clearly about both their desired outcome and the procedures for attaining the outcome are more likely to be successful. "A man is but a product of his thoughts. What he thinks he becomes."[23]

If the teacher desires for a student to be motivated, involved, and excited about the course material, then she will need to use these same traits to resolve the dispute. Juergensmeyer summarizes Gandhi's prescriptive advice about this important component of *satyagraha*: "She should employ her end as a means, in order for the means to become the end."[24]

IMPERFECT HERO

Gandhi was revered and worshipped by millions. Albert Einstein believed that "Generations to come, it may be, will scarce believe that such a one as this ever in flesh and blood walked upon this earth."[25] Gandhi was also reviled by many, who focused on his mistakes, quirks, and inconsistencies. Gandhi was open about his transgressions; as a child, he stole money from his father to buy cigarettes. He also ate meat, a violation of Hindi practices. Gandhi was not always a kind husband and supportive father. He suffered from anger, self-loathing, and harsh interactions. Gandhi was completely open about all of these shortcomings, believing everyone should know about his weaknesses and failures.

CONCLUSION

When Gandhi said that his message was his life, we are reminded of his enormous commitment to others as a public servant: "The best way to find yourself is to lose yourself in the service of others."[26] Gandhi experienced a great deal of clashing opinions, political corruption, detractors, and violence. Yet he remained optimistic: "You must not lose faith in humanity. Humanity is an ocean; if a few drops of the ocean are dirty, the ocean does not become dirty."[27]

When Gandhi said that his political beliefs were inseparable from his religion, he was talking about a spirituality based on action: "There are two days in the year that we cannot do anything, yesterday and tomorrow."[28] Gandhi's legacy provides meaningful inspiration for teachers: serve others; serve optimistically; use faith as motivation to action; use your own behavior as a model for what you hope others will be. Never give up: "Strength does not come from physical capacity. It comes from an indomitable will."[29] Gandhi concluded: "In a gentle way, you can shake the world."[30]

INTERSECTIONS

If humanity is to progress, Gandhi is inescapable. He lived, thought, and acted, inspired by the vision of humanity evolving toward a world of peace and harmony. We may ignore him at our own risk. Freedom is never voluntarily given by the oppressor; it must be demanded by the oppressed.

—Dr. Martin Luther King Jr.[31]

TEACHING SUMMARY: TEACH WITH "TRUTH FORCE" LIKE GANDHI

- Be the change you wish to see. Apply simple eternal truths to classroom situations.
- Be a joyful teacher.
- Return good for evil until the evildoer tires of evil. Take action against injustice.
- Creatively seek the truth about conflict, and the forces underlying the conflict.
- Seek solutions to difficulties through a process devoted to the truth.
- Maintain positive regard for all students in all situations.
- Recognize an injustice and confront it; battle creatively and cleanly; do not resort to violence.
- Use your ends (objectives) and your means (process) for the means to become the end.
- Be open about mistakes and shortcomings. Forgive as quickly and generously as possible.
- Be a teacher of action.

NOTES

1. WisdomQuotes, "460 Quotes."
2. Biography.com, "15 Quotes."
3. Sharp, *Moral Power*, 4.

4. WisdomQuotes, "460 Quotes."
5. Guha, *Gandhi*, 890.
6. Fischer, *Gandhi*, 61.
7. WisdomQuotes, "460 Quotes."
8. Nagler, *Nonviolence*.
9. WisdomQuotes, "460 Quotes."
10. WisdomQuotes, "460 Quotes."
11. Holy Bible, Matthew 5:44.
12. WisdomQuotes, "460 Quotes."
13. WisdomQuotes, "460 Quotes."
14. WisdomQuotes, "460 Quotes."
15. WisdomQuotes, "460 Quotes."
16. Jurgensmeyer, *Gandhi's Way*.
17. Jurgensmeyer, *Gandhi's Way*, 4.
18. WisdomQuotes, "460 Quotes."
19. Gandhi, *Young India*. May 7, 1931.
20. Weiner, *Socrates Express*, 164.
21. WisdomQuotes, "460 Quotes."
22. Jurgensmeyer, *Gandhi's Way*, 39–40.
23. Biography.com, "15 Quotes."
24. Jurgensmeyer, *Gandhi's Way*, 40.
25. Einstein, *Later Years*, 240.
26. Biography.com, "15 Quotes."
27. WisdomQuotes, "460 Quotes."
28. WisdomQuotes, "460 Quotes."
29. WisdomQuotes, "460 Quotes."
30. Biography, "15 Quotes."
31. Dalal, "Inescapable."

REFERENCES

Bhagavad-Gita: Krishnas's Counsel in Time of War. New York: Bantam Classics, 1986.

Biography.com. "15 Inspiring Gandhi Quotes." Updated October 1, 2020. Accessed February 25, 2021. https://www.biography.com/news/gandhi-quotes

Dalal, Rakhi. "If Humanity is to Progress, Gandhi is Inescapable." In *Life/Philosophy*. October 21, 2020. Accessed 14 January 2021. https://countercurrents.org/

Einstein, Albert. *Out of My Later Years*. New York: Citadel Press, 1956.

Fischer, Louis. *Gandhi: His Life and Message for the World*. New York: Mentor, 1954.

Gandhi, M.K., Editor. *Young India*. May 7, 1931. Ahmedabad, India.

Guha, Ramachandra. *Gandhi: The Years that Changed the World, 1914-1948*. New York: Vintage, 2018.

"Holy Bible." New Living Translation. Carol Stream, IL: Tyndale, 1996.

Juergensmeyer, Mark. *Gandhi's Way: A Handbook of Conflict Resolution*. Berkeley, CA: University of California Press, 2005.

Nagler, Michael N. *The Nonviolence Handbook: A Guide for Practical Action*. Oakland, CA: Berrett-Koehler Publishers, 2014.

Sharp, Gene. *Gandhi Wields the Weapon of Moral Power*. Ahmedabad, India: Navjivan Trust, 1997.

Weiner, Eric. *The Socrates Express: In Search of Life Lessons from Dead Philosophers*. New York: Simon & Schuster, 2020.

WisdomQuotes. "460 Mahatma Gandhi Quotes." Updated February 15, 2021. Accessed February 25, 2021. https://wisdomquotes.com/gandhi-quotes/

Chapter 10

Enthusiasm under Adversity

Anne Frank

Figure 10.1 Anne Frank. *Source*: Wikimedia Commons. File: Anne Frank lacht naar de schoolfotograaf.jpg.

A person who's happy will make others happy; a person who has courage and faith will never die in misery!

—Anne Frank[1]

How wonderful it is that no one has to wait, but can start right now to gradually change the world! How wonderful it is that everyone, great and small, can immediately help bring about justice by giving of themselves! . . . You can always—always—give something, even if it's a simple act of kindness!

—Anne Frank[2]

CHAPTER SYNOPSIS

Anne Frank and her family lived under confinement in a secret annex in Amsterdam to avoid capture by the Nazis while she was thirteen to fifteen years old. Her wise, insightful, and inspirational diary entries illuminate how teachers can successfully navigate life during confinement, or other difficult times. Anne's pervasive optimism and courage are explored, with special attention to the implications for remote teaching and learning. Anne's exuberant life is used to illustrate good teaching practices in times of difficulty. Anne Frank's extraordinary diary provides lessons for continuous self-improvement, optimism, and courage for educators.

Anne Frank was born in Germany on June 12, 1929, to Otto Frank and Edith Hollander Frank. Anne's father served in the German Army during World War I, and prospered after the war as a banker and manufacturer of cough lozenges. The family had lived in Frankfurt for generations, enjoying a comfortable lifestyle that included frequent social activities, entertainment, and a large community of friends.

The world economy crashed in 1929, about the same time that Anne was born. The financial hardship of the Great Depression in Germany and Austria led to social unrest, creating the conditions that led to the rise of Adolph Hitler and the National Socialist Party, commonly called the Nazis. Hitler blamed the Jewish people for the difficulties in Germany and Austria. As the economic crisis worsened, the blame intensified, and Hitler acquired more power. In 1933, Hitler became Chancellor of Germany and immediately called for a boycott of all Jewish businesses and banned Jews from government employment. Anne and her family were Jewish.

When Anne was four years old, Otto Frank and his family emigrated from Frankfurt to Amsterdam, along with many Jews seeking a way out of the increasingly repressive and dangerous situation in Germany. Anne moved into an apartment in Amsterdam with her parents and older sister Margot. Margot was polite and respectful to her parents and other adults. Anne was extraordinarily talkative, intelligent, opinionated, and joyously unrestrained. Anne bluntly assessed herself and her sister: "Margot is . . . such a goody-goody, perfection itself, but I seem to have enough mischief in me for the two of us put together."[3]

Anne and Margot quickly adjusted to life in Amsterdam. Their father became successful again, with a new business that produced a jelling agent for making jams. We know a great deal about Anne Frank because she kept a diary, where she recorded all of her thoughts, ideas, dreams, difficulties, and youthful contradictions. Anne wrote about her strong feelings about most people, ideas, and events. The diary was given to Anne as a gift on her thirteenth birthday. On the inside cover, Anne wrote, "I hope I will be able to confide everything to you, as I have never been able to confide in anyone, and I hope you will be a great source of comfort and support."[4]

By 1942, eight years after the Franks had moved to Amsterdam, the Nazis had brutally attacked and conquered many European nations and people, including the Netherlands. Worse yet, the Nazi leadership finalized a plan to exterminate all European Jews. All Jewish people in Holland were forced to register with the German authorities and wear yellow stars sewn on their clothing marked with the word "Jood" (Jew).

One month after Anne received her diary, a letter arrived from the government ordering Margot to report to a labor camp. To avoid being sent to the Nazi camps, the family immediately went into hiding in a secret annex in the back of a house in Amsterdam. Four additional Jewish refugees joined the Frank family in the secret annex to avoid round-up and deportation.

Anne continued writing in her diary for the next two years, recording thoughts and emotions common for a girl of her age. Also recorded were numerous uncommon ideas: her entries are wise, insightful, and inspirational. Anne's profound writing has made her a global hero, inspiring millions with her optimism, courage, and self-awareness well beyond her years.

The diary comes to an abrupt end on August 1, 1944, the day that Anne and her family were arrested and sent to concentration camps. Someone whose identity is still unknown had revealed the Frank family's location to the authorities. Anne, her sister Margot, and her mother Edith died while imprisoned due to the horrible health, sanitary, physical, and emotional conditions in the camps. Miraculously, Anne's father Otto survived and returned to Amsterdam when the war was over.

After Anne's arrest, a family friend collected the pages of the diary, and returned them to Otto when he returned. Anne's father shared *The Diary of*

Anne Frank with the world with the hope that her story would cause reflection on the Holocaust and action for humanity to avoid such tragedies in the future. Anne Frank, a writer of a single book written at age thirteen to fifteen, is now a beacon of hope, courage, and determination for all who hear her story and read her diary.

COURAGE

Anne, her family, and the four additional occupants of the annex lived under wartime conditions that are impossible to fully comprehend for those who have never experienced the extreme and ever-present fear sustained over a long period of time. On July 11, 1942, Anne recorded, "I can't tell you how oppressive it is *never* to be able to go outdoors, also I'm very afraid that we will be discovered and be shot."[5]

The Franks were fully aware that during their confinement many Jews from their community were rounded up and sent to holding facilities at Westerbork, used as a staging ground for deportation of Jews to concentration camps further east. At Auschwitz and other concentration camps, almost all of the Jews and political prisoners were put to death in gas chambers upon arrival.[6]

Given the horrible consequences of being found out, the annex occupants devised strict rules of behavior to avoid discovery and capture: "We have to whisper and tread lightly during the day, otherwise the people in the warehouse might hear us."[7] Coughing, talking, looking out the window, and flushing the toilet were not permitted during daylight hours. Tragically, Anne's fears of capture became reality. Although her life was spared from the gas chambers at Auschwitz, Anne was transferred to Bergen-Belsen, another concentration camp, where she died of spotted typhoid fever in early 1945.

Anne did not succumb to fear even though it was present throughout her captivity. Anne and her family survived the difficult, tense claustrophobia of living in a confined space without relief for over two years. Anne's high spirits and sense of humor sustained her through the dark times: "The 'Secret Annexe' is an ideal hiding place. Although it leans to one side and is damp, you'd never find such a comfortable hiding place anywhere in Amsterdam, no, perhaps not even in the whole of Holland."[8] Another source of fear was German bombing missions: "We've just had a third air raid, I clenched my teeth together to make myself feel courageous."[9]

With more time spent in confinement, Anne's positive attitude begins to shine through her challenging situation: "I've often been downcast, but never in despair. I regard our hiding as a dangerous adventure, romantic and interesting at the same time. In my diary I treat all the privations as amusing."[10]

Anne's uncanny positive attitude can be applied to a broad range of situations. Many experts consider positivity to be a prerequisite to success in any activity, pursuit, or career.

Optimists such as Anne believe that they have control over their attitude and circumstances. Optimists also believe that their problems are short-lived and specific to the situation. Pessimists perceive difficulties and roadblocks as permanent and out of their control. This difference in world view causes optimists to take action to improve their situations. Coauthors John Luckner, an educator, and Suzanne Rudolph, a psychologist, write that, "Pessimistic or negative thinking can undermine our sense of confidence and our ability to cope and impair our performance."[11]

OPTIMISM

Teachers can benefit from reflection on Anne Frank's life, as well as the crimes and injustices forced upon her, her family, and her people. Anne is noted for her optimistic view of the inherent goodness of all people in spite of her dire situation. American writer and philosopher Ralph Waldo Emerson wrote, "Nothing great was ever achieved without enthusiasm."[12] When there is trouble in our world, nation, or community, Anne's optimism shows the way.

If a teacher can share optimism when students and colleagues are struggling or worried, a great gift has been bestowed upon those persons. Learning how to be enthusiastic is essential for anyone in a leadership position, whether it be parenting, teaching, a volunteer role, or an elected position. Enthusiasm can be learned through practice: replacing negative thoughts with optimistic ones can revolutionize a teacher's effectiveness. It can also improve the teacher's life.

From years of teaching experience, Luckner and Rudolph have found that "Successful teachers convey a sense of confidence in their knowledge and in their ability to teach. By being enthusiastic, speaking clearly, answering questions with assurance, being decisive, and admitting when you don't know the answer or when you have made a mistake, you demonstrate the quality of a successful, confident teacher."[13] Confidence is built on a foundation of knowledge, coupled with efforts to maintain optimism and enthusiasm.

Like optimists, successful teachers view setbacks as temporary. Roadblocks are seen as opportunities to conquer and learn from. When difficulties arise in the classroom or other teaching activities, the teacher who adopts Anne Frank's world view can make a positive difference in the world.

In a lecture to college students, former President George W. Bush shared his experience with leadership: "You can't lead the nation, you can't make good decisions unless you're optimistic about the future. . . . Imagine somebody saying, follow me, the world is going to be worse. That's not a very good organizing principle about which to lead people."[14] Reading, re-reading, and reflecting on this statement can be productive for all citizens, especially teachers.

Teachers can immediately adopt Bush's simple leadership philosophy with great results. For individuals struggling with positivity, try it for just one hour, then expand your efforts, to one day, and see how long you can maintain positive thoughts, statements, and actions. For many, positivity requires practice. Like any meaningful activity, the more effort teachers put into optimism, the better the results.

Bush continued, "I'm optimistic about our future, and the reason I am is because I believe so strongly in what America stands for: liberty and freedom and human rights, and the human dignity of every single person."[15] Bush's timely and important second statement is also worthy of contemplation in the context of Anne's life experience and the Holocaust. Teachers can benefit from revisiting their original motivation for becoming a teacher, and their reasons for continuing to teach. Reflection on the importance of teaching can result in renewed energy and enthusiasm for helping students to learn, grow, and prosper.

At times during her confinement, Anne struggled: "My nerves often get the better of me, especially on Sundays, that's when I really feel miserable."[16] Anne was not continuously happy and optimistic throughout her confinement, but she realized that the negative feelings were not permanent, and within her control to change: "I wander from one room to another, downstairs and up again, feeling like a songbird whose wings have been clipped and who is hurling himself in utter darkness against the bars of his cage."[17]

Living under the threat of death at the hands of the Nazis was not easy, yet Anne always regained her enthusiasm for life after periods of difficulty. She later wrote, "I have lots of courage, I always feel so strong and as if I can bear a great deal, I feel so free and so young! I was glad when I first realized it because I don't think I shall easily bow down before the blows that inevitably come to everyone."[18] Anne's simple advice is timely and relevant.

MINDFULNESS

Anne Frank reported: "I have an outstanding trait in my character, which must strike anyone who knows me for any length of time, and that is my knowledge of myself. I can watch myself and my actions, just like an outsider."[19] Anne writes that her self-knowledge allows her to face herself without prejudice and without making excuses. Anne is able to observe what is good and bad about her behavior, and self-correct the actions that she finds undesirable.

Anne was ahead of her time in promoting self-awareness and self-care. Luckner and Rudolph suggest that "one way to increase optimism and emotional well-being is through the practice of mindfulness."[20] Mindfulness is the ability to be aware of, and conscious of, your thoughts, feelings, and behaviors in the present moment in a nonreactive way, rather than responding to events on automatic pilot or out of old habits.

Anne wrote: "I know my own faults and shortcomings better than anyone, but the difference is that I also know that I want to improve, shall improve, and have already improved a great deal."[21] Enthusiasm defeated Anne's difficulties. Bill Ayers agrees: "If teachers are never self-critical, they will lose their capacity for renewal and growth. They will become self-justifying and dogmatic. On the other side, if teachers are too self-critical, they become powerless and timid."[22]

One of Anne Frank's brilliant insights for teachers is that if you believe that you are doing important work, you will be happier in your personal life, and more productive in your professional life. The Dalai Lama suggests that teachers look for evidence that demonstrates that teaching is valuable, worthwhile, important, and rewarding. When people believe that their work serves a higher purpose, they are more satisfied, productive, and capable.[23]

Writing became an essential part of Anne's life and identity. She wrote, "And if I haven't any talent for writing books or newspaper articles, well, then I can always write for myself. I want to go on living even after my death! And therefore I am grateful to God for giving me this gift, this possibility of developing myself and of writing, of expressing all that is in me."[24]

Anne consistently practiced gratitude throughout her confinement. "Every day I feel that I am developing inwardly, that the liberation is drawing nearer and how beautiful nature is, how good the people are about me, how interesting the adventure is! Why, then, should I be in despair?"[25]

ONLINE TEACHING

People who experience unspeakable difficulties often benefit from keeping a consistent routine. Anne's diary describes how the occupants of the secret annex made it through their days. Regulation, routine, and disciplined regimentation provided relief from the terrifying unknown. The occupants' maintained a rigid schedule of activities and strictly adhered to a daily routine. Specific times during each day were allotted for meals, rest, baths, and daily exercise. Reading was an important part of the day, as was humor. This straightforward strategy provides teachers with an exemplary guide for teaching during a crisis, and remote teaching and learning.

When teaching remotely, a great deal of communication is lost without in-person contact. The foundation of successful online teaching can be found by following the example of the occupants of the secret annex: organization, routine, consistency, optimism, and communication. This strategy for online teaching differs from the strategy for face-to-face classroom teaching. For traditional in-person classes, a diversity of styles, routines, and classroom assessments can keep students interested. In distance learning, students seek and require great organization, regularity, and rapid communication to eliminate uncertainty.

Successful online classes are built on a solid platform of consistent content delivery, routine assessments with an unchanging format, and timely response to student questions, concerns, and issues. The Frank family implemented a high degree of organization within the annex to make their lives more bearable under the unrelenting strain. Teachers can follow this example by providing online course material in a useful, organized, and streamlined fashion.

Online learners have a strong preference for routine; constancy; regularity; and desire for control over their learning environment. Teachers who provide this type of structured, consistent learning environment will be rewarded by a more effective class, and by greater levels of student learning and comprehension. Elimination of all uncertainty through regimented regularity will create a solid online environment.

CONCLUSION

Anne manifested an amazing ability to learn and grow while in captivity in a highly compromised learning environment. One of the major themes of her diary is that of personal growth and self-improvement. Keeping a diary allowed Anne to reread, reflect on, and rewrite earlier entries. Anne changed a great deal in the two years under confinement. One change in attitude resulted from thinking critically about herself. Anne changed her opinions of her mother and the Van Dams, a family that shared the secret annex with the Franks.

Originally, Anne was highly critical and unforgiving about the Van Dams, but with reflection, she changed her mind: "Until now I was immovable! I always thought the Van Dams were in the wrong, but we too are partly to blame. . . . I hope that I have acquired a bit of insight and will use it well when the occasion arises."[26]

Not only did Anne worry about her relationships, but she strongly desired to be lovable and loved. Anne's keen self-awareness allowed her to speak honestly about her wants and needs: "The whole time I've been here I've longed unconsciously—and at times consciously—for trust, love, and physical affection."[27]

Most students, and most people, share this emotional need and desire to be heard, respected, and loved for who they are. Bill Ayers reflects, "Teaching is still a powerful calling for many people, and powerful for the same reasons that it has always been so. There are still young people who need a thoughtful, caring adult in their lives; someone who can nurture and challenge them, who can coach and guide, understand and care about them."[28]

When teachers take time and effort to really listen to students, to more fully understand who they are, and what their wants, needs, desires, goals, and struggles are . . . a better foundation for learning is made, leading to better, deeper understanding of the world, and more student success in their class and throughout their life and career.

Teachers can also benefit from keeping a diary, or recording their observations. Journaling provides an effective way to remember desired changes in lectures, presentations, assignments, and assessments. Anne provides an amazing tool for self-improvement: "How noble and good everyone could be if, every evening before falling asleep, they were to recall to their minds the events of the whole day and consider exactly what has been good and bad. Then without realizing it, you try to improve yourself at the start of each new day."[29]

Like most important ideas about personal development, Anne's pragmatic tool is simple, yet enormously impactful if utilized. Anne Frank not only survived a difficult time, she thrived under adversity. She provides enormous inspiration to sharing joy and enthusiasm with students. Good teachers, like Anne Frank, always seek to improve by challenging themselves to greater levels of self-awareness and optimism.

INTERSECTIONS

Her story means a lot. It's profound.

—Bob Dylan on Anne Frank[30]

I read the diary before I went to prison, but reading books at that time was something totally different from reading the same book inside prison, especially that of Anne Frank because we identified with her in the situation which we were in and therefore the lessons of her tragedy sunk more deeply in our souls and also encouraged us in our situation.

—Nelson Mandela, in the documentary,
"The Diary on Robben Island."[31]

*The victory of the democratic forces in South Africa is a contribution
to this world-wide effort to rid humanity of the evil of racism. It is Anne
Frank's victory. It is an achievement of humanity as a whole.*

—Nelson Mandela at the opening of the Anne Frank
Exhibition at Museum Africa, Johannesburg.[32]

TEACHING SUMMARY: BE OPTIMISTIC
LIKE ANNE FRANK

- Choose to be courageous and confident in the classroom, especially during difficult times and situations. Students and colleagues will respect you, and follow your lead.
- Seek to find the inherent goodness of all students no matter what they have done.
- Be unrelentingly enthusiastic about teaching content, pedagogy, students, and life!
- Use self-awareness to improve your teaching and influence on students: reflect on how your actions and behaviors influence outcomes.
- Keep a diary or journal to record what went right and what could be improved. Read and reflect often.
- Follow Anne Frank's simple plan for continuous self-improvement: review your behavior at the end of each day by weighing the rights and wrongs. You will automatically do better at the start of each new day.

NOTES

1. Frank, *Diary*, June 6, 1944, 211.
2. Frank, "Give!" March 26, 1944, 88.
3. Frank, *Diary*, September 27, 1942, 31.
4. Frank, *Diary*, June 12, 1942, inside front cover.
5. Frank, *Diary*, July 11, 1942, 21.
6. United States Holocaust Memorial Museum, "Westerbork."
7. Frank, *Diary*, July 11, 1942, 21.
8. Frank, *Diary*, July 11, 1942, 20.
9. Frank, *Diary*, August 3, 1943, 95.
10. Frank, *Diary*, May 3, 1944, 223.
11. Luckner and Rudolph, *Teach Well*, 6.
12. Emerson, "Circles."
13. Luckner and Rudolph, *Teach Well*, 178.
14. Bush, *Landon Lecture*.

15. Bush, *Landon Lecture.*
16. Frank, *Diary*, October 29, 1943, 113.
17. Frank, *Diary*, October 29, 1943, 113.
18. Frank, *Diary*, July 15, 1944, 260.
19. Frank, *Diary*, July 15, 1944, 260.
20. Luckner and Rudolph, *Teach Well*, 6.
21. Frank, *Diary*, June 14, 1944, 248.
22. Ayers, *To Teach*, 144.
23. The Dalai Lama and Cutler, *Happiness*; Luckner and Rudolph, *Teach Well*, 7.
24. Frank, *Diary*, April 14, 1944, 197.
25. Frank, *Diary*, May 3, 1944, 223–224.
26. Frank, *Diary*, January 22, 1944, 140.
27. Frank, *Diary*, April 14, 1944, 197.
28. Ayers, *To Teach*, 20.
29. Frank, *Diary*, comment on January 22, 1944, 61.
30. Brinkley, *Bob Dylan.*
31. Mandela, "Interview."
32. Mandela, "Remarks."

REFERENCES

Ayers, William. *To Teach: The Journey of a Teacher*. Third Edition. New York: Teachers College Press, 2010.

Brinkley, Douglas. "Bob Dylan Has a Lot on His Mind." *New York Times*, June 12, 2020. https://www.nytimes.com/2020/06/12/arts/music/bob-dylan-rough-and-rowdy-ways.html

Bush, George W. "Landon Lecture." Landon Lecture Series on Public Issues. Kansas State University, Manhattan, Kansas. January 23, 2006. Accessed April 29, 2021. https://www.k-state.edu/landon/speakers/georgew-bush/transcript.html

The Dalai Lama and Howard C. Cutler. *The Art of Happiness at Work*. New York: Riverhead, 2003.

Emerson, Ralph Waldo. "Circles." 1841. Ralph Waldo Emerson website. Accessed April 29, 2021. https://emersoncentral.com/texts/essays-first-series/circles

Frank, Anne. *The Diary of a Young Girl*. Translated by B. M. Mooyaart-Doubleday. Garden City, NJ: Doubleday, 1952.

Frank, Anne. "Give! Sunday, March 26, 1944." In *Anne Frank's Tales from the Secret Annex: A Collection of Her Short Stories, Fables, and Lesser-Known Writings*, edited by Gerrold van der Stroom and Susan Massotty, translated by Susan Massotty, 85–88. New York: Bantam, 2008.

Frank, Otto. "Memories of Anne." Typescript 1968. Anne Frank House website. Accessed April 29, 2021. https://www.annefrank.org/en/anne-frank/diary/

Luckner, John, and Suzanne Rudolph. *Teach Well, Live Well: Strategies for Success*. Thousand Oaks, CA: Corwin, 2009.

Mandela, Nelson. "Interview for Documentary Het Achterhuis op Robbeneiland (The Diary on Robben Island)." Interview by Dutch broadcasting cooperation VARA, May 4, 1995.

Mandela, Nelson. "Remarks at the Opening of the Anne Frank Exhibition at Museum Africa." Johannesburg, South Africa, August 15, 1994. *Nelson Mandela Foundation.* Accessed April 27 2021. http://atom.nelsonmandela.org/index.php/za-com-mr-s-188

US Holocaust Memorial Museum. Holocaust Encyclopedia "Westerbork." Accessed April 29, 2021. https://encyclopedia.ushmm.org/content/en/article/westerbork

Chapter 11

Courage from Conviction

Martin Luther King, Jr.

Figure 11.1 **Martin Luther King, Jr.** *Source*: Wikimedia Commons. USMC-09611.jpg.

The time is always right to do what is right.

—Martin Luther King, Jr.[1]

If you can't fly then run, if you can't run then walk, if you can't walk
then crawl, but whatever you do you have to keep moving forward.

—Martin Luther King, Jr.[2]

CHAPTER SYNOPSIS

Martin Luther King, Jr. was a visionary thinker, powerful speaker, and effective activist with important lessons for teachers about how to make the world a better place. During his life, King faced both adulation and fierce hatred. King's life and career are examined to illustrate courage in the face of fierce opposition, inspiring teachers to fight their fear, and continue in the face of adversity. Educators are encouraged to identify the underlying motivation and purpose for their work, enabling them to teach courageously and with conviction.

Martin Luther King, Jr. was a leader in the 1960s US civil rights movement. Through sermons, speeches, writings, and nonviolent protest, Dr. King brought lasting change to oppressed people. His progress in bringing justice and equality to all races was not universally supported. Dr. King was assassinated on April 4, 1968. He was thirty-nine years old.

On the night before he was killed in Memphis, Tennessee, Dr. King shared a message of hope for others: "I would like to live a long life. . . . But I'm not concerned about that now. I just want to do God's will. And He's allowed me to go up to the mountain. And I've looked over, and I've seen the promised land. I may not get there with you. But I want you to know tonight, that we, as a people, will get to the promised land. . . . Say that I was a drum major for justice. Say that I was a drum major for peace. I was a drum major for righteousness."[3]

Dr. King's final speech is shockingly bleak. However, it is also remarkably hopeful. Dr. King explained that his life was sacrificial, passing on the fight for justice to others. This powerful oratory was characteristic of Dr. King. He seemed to know that he was soon to be assassinated. His unequalled courage and power as a leader came from his unrelenting work for social justice and hope for a better future, in spite of opponents who desired his death.

Dr. King led a movement that had a lasting positive impact on the United States in the face of death threats to him and his family. What was the source of this deep level of bravery, commitment, and success? In his final speech, Martin Luther King, Jr. provided an answer: "When people get caught up with that which is right and they are willing to sacrifice for it, there is no stopping point short of victory."[4] What an inspiration for educators: doing the right thing will result in powerful personal and professional outcomes!

Martin Luther King, Jr. was born to Martin Luther King, Sr. and Alberta Williams in 1929 in Atlanta, Georgia. Alberta was the daughter of A.D. Williams, pastor of Atlanta's Ebenezer Baptist Church from 1894 to 1931. Martin Sr. was pastor at Ebenezer from 1931 to 1975. Martin's childhood was comfortable, and his parents were well respected in their Atlanta community. However, economic success did not protect African Americans from severe racism, discrimination, and segregation.

Martin became aware of racism at age six, when the father of his white friend told his son that he could no longer play with Martin because of his race. "I was greatly shocked, and from that moment on I was determined to hate every white person."[5]

In response, Martin's parents shared their belief that it was their Christian duty to love the friend's white father, in spite of his views and actions. Martin wondered, "How could I love a race of people who hated me and who had been responsible for breaking me up with one of my best childhood friends?"[6] This question unsettled Martin throughout his childhood. He later came to agree with his parents' teachings that he should love his enemies.

Atlanta was deeply segregated during Martin's childhood. Schools, swimming pools, parks, theaters, restaurants, and stores were for either whites or blacks, but not both. After spending a summer in Connecticut, Martin returned to Atlanta on a segregated train. "The very idea of separation did something to my sense of dignity and self-respect."[7] Based on these early experiences and many other childhood encounters with oppression, Martin would devote his life to the elimination of racism and segregation from the United States.

Martin was a highly intelligent, precocious, and thoughtful young man. He skipped two grades in high school, entered Morehouse College at age fifteen, where he earned a bachelor's degree in sociology at age nineteen. Dr. King felt called to the ministry, and entered Crozer Theological Seminary in Pennsylvania in 1948. "My call to the ministry was not a miraculous or supernatural something. On the contrary it was an inner urge calling me to serve humanity."[8] While a student at Crozer, Dr. King attended a lecture on Gandhi, and became deeply interested in Gandhi's teachings in nonviolent resistance: "My study of Gandhi convinced me that true pacifism is not nonresistance to evil, but nonviolent resistance to evil. Between the two positions, there is a world of difference. Gandhi resisted evil with as much vigor and power as the violent resister, but he resisted with love instead of hate."[9] Gandhi's views are explored in chapter 9.

Martin continued to excel in school and received his Bachelor of Divinity degree at Crozer and a doctorate in systematic theology at Boston University in 1955. While in Boston, Martin met and married Coretta Scott from Marion, Alabama. The Kings had two sons and two daughters. Coretta provided strong support for Martin through both good and bad times.

Dr. King sought nothing short of improvement of the human condition using nonviolent action that included boycotts, protests, and marches. His leadership of the Civil Rights Movement was eventually successful, resulting in enactment of the Civil Rights Act of 1964, which prohibited discrimination, and the Voting Rights Act of 1965, which outlawed discriminatory voting practices. Dr. King combined Christian ideals with Gandhi's operational techniques. Dr. King's work is an astonishing example of what can be accomplished when an individual has a strong purpose and the courage to act.

Due to his leadership role in nonviolent protests, Dr. King was arrested over twenty times, physically assaulted several times, had his family home bombed, and lived with continuous death threats. For his courageous service, Dr. King was awarded five honorary degrees, he was *Time* magazine's "Man of the Year" in 1963, and he became not only a major leader of the civil rights movement but also a world figure. Dr. King's work also led to the Nobel Peace Prize.

INTERCONNECTEDNESS

A persistent theme of Dr. King's sermons, speeches, and writing reflects ties that bind people of every race, ethnicity, background, financial status, and nationality. This connectedness of all people is brilliantly shared in King's celebrated "Letter from a Birmingham Jail." The letter was written in 1963, when Dr. King was arrested for protesting the poor treatment of African Americans in Birmingham, Alabama.

In his letter, Dr. King told his opponents, "You deplore the demonstrations taking place in Birmingham. But your statement, I am sorry to say, fails to express a similar concern for the conditions that brought about the demonstrations. . . . Injustice anywhere is a threat to justice everywhere. We are caught in an inescapable network of mutuality, tied in a single garment of destiny. Whatever affects one directly, affects all indirectly."[10]

The idea of interconnectedness is familiar to educators. The overall success of a lecture, classroom presentation, or student activity depends strongly on the entire class, and each individual student. A single student dissenter, troublemaker, sleeper, or talker affects the teacher and the other students. A teacher's ability to concentrate without distraction is a prerequisite to a good presentation. A student's ability to listen and react to a classroom presentation is also an essential condition for student learning. Likewise, group projects and activities rely on each individual's contribution.

Students can have positive and negative effects on the entire class. Awareness of the interconnectedness of all students provides teachers with an opportunity to enhance classroom climate, productivity, and efficiency. Students who interrupt classroom presentations or activities limit all students learning. Students with a positive attitude can have a large, constructive impact on surrounding students. Student-teacher relationships can be usefully thought of as the sum of all positive and negative interactions between all students and the instructor.

Lack of knowledge or experience with people of divergent backgrounds can result in poor relations. Dr. King, the preacher, explained, "Men often hate each other because they fear each other; they fear each other because they don't know each other; they don't know each other because they can not communicate; they can not communicate because they are separated."[11] Educators who spend time with people who are different from themselves can reduce the fear and hatred associated with the unknown. When fear and hatred are diminished through shared experience, student learning outcomes are enhanced.

TENSION

Dr. King's approach to catalyzing social change for justice was nonviolent. The civil rights movement, however, was one of confrontation: "My citing the creation of tension as part of the work of the nonviolent resister may sound rather shocking. But I must confess that I am not afraid of the word, 'tension.' I have earnestly opposed violent tension, but there is a type of constructive, nonviolent tension which is necessary for growth."[12]

Dr. King did not shy away from opposition. Instead, he analyzed the strengths and weaknesses of all arguments, ideas, and objections: "The function of education . . . is to teach one to think intensively and to think critically. . . . Intelligence plus character—that is the goal of true education."[13] Creating tension is how both activism and education work. New knowledge requires change, and change can be controversial. Learning new ideas can take students out of their comfort zone. Just as Dr. King's nonviolent action created tension that led to negotiation, education also requires tension between new and old ideas that leads to critical thinking.

Teachers can productively follow Dr. King's path by choosing and implementing strategies for maximum learning impact. Sharing factual knowledge in an unbiased manner is a nonaggressive teaching approach that is similar to nonviolent social change promoted by Gandhi and Dr. King. Constructive nonviolent tension is necessary for positive change and growth.

Dr. King believed that strong adherence to nonviolence was likely to be more successful than violence. In his Nobel Prize Lecture, Dr. King explained, "Violence as a way of achieving racial justice is both impractical and immoral. I am not unmindful of the fact that violence often brings about momentary results. Nations have frequently won their independence in battle. But in spite of temporary victories, violence never brings permanent peace."[14] Similarly, teachers who introduce new ideas in an aggressive or challenging fashion may not be as effective as teachers who carefully consider instructional methods that meet students where they are.

Dr. King's nonviolent actions required enormous planning, thought, adjustment, and evaluation. The success of the civil rights movement was built on continuous efforts to bring divergent groups together. Many of Dr. King's actions were not successful. Dr. King met opposition when he attempted to fight racial injustice and housing segregation in Chicago in 1966. Bottles and bricks were thrown at the demonstrators, and Dr. King was struck by a rock. While Dr. King was disappointed to be unable to contribute to positive change in Chicago, he viewed the march as a learning experience, and believed that his work led to change later on.

Dr. King's ability to move forward in the face of setbacks, roadblocks, and difficulties is unparalleled. He had the supreme ability to persevere, to meet new challenges, and to change his goals, strategies, and ideas with changes in social conditions.

HOPE

Dr. King desired to bring drastic social change to an imperfect nation. He was a visionary leader and change agent, resulting in strong opposition. Dr. King was viewed by many as an "extremist." He was repeatedly arrested, jailed, and assaulted. He received an endless stream of credible death threats. His family home was bombed in 1956 during a bus boycott in Montgomery, Alabama. In 1959, he was nearly killed by a Harlem stabbing. His chosen career path was difficult, dangerous, and ultimately deadly. Dr. King viewed it as his duty to expose himself to violence, to promote racial justice.

Dr. King viewed the challenges of the social change movement as temporary. Dr. King's unwavering optimism can provide a foundation for effective teaching. Students are forgiving of mistakes, oversights, misjudgments, and virtually all errors if their teacher does not give up on them or the learning process. When problems arise, teachers can look to the future with the same optimism that Dr. King shared with his congregation and his followers: "We must accept finite disappointment, but we must never lose infinite hope."[15]

Through his words, actions, and beliefs, he communicated to oppressed people everywhere that "you are somebody."

Teachers who bring Dr. King's affirmation, encouragement, and support to all students will share the immense joy of helping others. For many teachers, helping students is the purpose behind their life and career. In particular, students who are facing difficulties or low self-esteem can be supported using Dr. King's personalized model of doing everything possible to move the world in the right direction. When a leader or teacher provides individual attention to students, hope and optimism is shared and spread with amazing consequences.

Perhaps the most powerful of Dr. King's teachings is the admonition to meet hatred with love. After a bomb was thrown into Dr. King's house in Montgomery on January 30, 1956, a crowd of his supporters gathered in the front of the damaged home. They were angry; many sought retribution. Some brandished baseball bats, knives, and guns. Dr. King's response shocked his angry followers: "We must meet violence with nonviolence. . . . We must love our white brothers, no matter what they do to us. We must make them know that we love them. . . . We must meet hate with love."[16]

This heroic demonstration of discipline is useful to educators in two ways. First, teachers need to look no further to find an example of doing the right thing. Practicing forgiveness with others becomes easier when recalling Dr. King's extraordinary response to hatred. Second, the magnitude of typical teaching trials can be put into perspective when thinking about the continual opposition faced by Dr. King. Bombs. Assaults. Death threats. Teaching difficulties rarely rise to this level, and teachers can look to Dr. King's strength, conviction, and courage to continue forward to combat and defeat their challenges.

Dr. King was criticized during his life by many people for many things: moving forward too quickly, not moving forward quickly enough, communist beliefs, opposition to the Vietnam War, and extramarital affairs, to name a few. The FBI was determined to reduce Dr. King's substantial influence and power. The intense public scrutiny placed on Dr. King by his opponents caused him great distress for many years. Dr. King was human.

Dr. King's strength and courage allowed him to overcome his anxiety, guilt, and depression toward the end of his life. By his final speech in Memphis, the night before he was killed, Dr. King had found mercy: "In the final analysis, God does not judge us by the separate incidents or the separate mistakes that we make, but by the total bent of our lives. In the final analysis, God knows that his children are weak and they are frail. In the final analysis, what God requires is that your heart is right."[17]

As with all teachers, students, and the twelve teaching heroes in this book, Dr. King was flawed. Hours before his death, he extended his substantial ability to forgive others to himself: "You don't need to go out saying that Martin Luther King is a saint. Oh, no. I want you to know this morning that I'm a sinner like all of God's children. But I want to be a good man. And I want to hear a voice saying to me one day, 'I take you in and I bless you, because you tried. It is well that it was within thine heart.'"[18]

Educators, like many professionals, frequently suffer from self-criticism, doubt, and remorse. Dedicated teachers seek perfection in all that they do, and particularly in the strong desire to help students learn, grow, and thrive. All human activity is imperfect, which can cause great distress for teachers. Teachers who forgive themselves, as Dr. King suggested, from imperfections, mistakes, and errors in judgement will be renewed, allowing them to provide greater service to others.

Dr. King had an enormous positive impact on the people of the world by doing the right thing repeatedly over the course of his life. Like all people, he struggled to always be "a good man." Teachers can productively follow Dr. King's example by moving past their personal struggles in the service of others.

MEANING AND PURPOSE

Dr. King's effectiveness and influence on social justice is exemplary, but his success came at a cost. The participants in the civil rights movement were subjected to abuse, oppression, violence, and in many cases, death. Dr. King and his allies needed courage to participate in nonviolent activities, and deep fearlessness to persist as danger and opposition mounted. Dr. King was fearless because his message was bigger than himself.

On August 28, 1963, an estimated 250,000 people participated in the March on Washington to advocate for the civil and economic rights of African Americans. Dr. King shared his personal aspirations in his keynote speech from the steps of the Lincoln Memorial: "I have a dream that one day this nation will rise up and live out the true meaning of its creed—we hold these truths to be self-evident that all men are created equal. . . . I have a dream that one day little black boys and girls will be holding hands with little white boys and girls."[19]

Service to others provides deep purpose, inspiration, and enthusiasm for teaching. All else springs from the merit of helping others: confidence, determination, courage, and effectiveness. Because Dr. King's goals were righteous, he was able to be arrested, face death threats, and be publicly disgraced without fear. Like Dr. King, if teachers know why they teach, they can be courageous, persistent, and constructive.

CONCLUSION

Dr. King stated, "Courage faces fear and thereby masters it."[20] One of the challenges of moving forward in the face of challenge is getting started. Dr.

King suggested, "Take the first step in faith. You don't have to see the whole staircase, just take the first step."[21] Inara Scott, the assistant dean for Teaching and Learning Excellence at Oregon State University, motivates pedagogical inclusivity: the inclusive mindset "reminds us that our job is to educate *all of our students*, which requires consciously considering whether all of our students have access to our content, our community, and our services."[22]

Scott provides a pathway for creating more inclusive classrooms based on personal reflection: "ask yourself why you do the work you do, your goals, and how your background and history may inform the person you bring into the classroom. Consider how your background may differ from your students, and where you may overlap."[23]

Scott summarizes the literature on inclusive teaching and inclusive pedagogy: "1. Students learn more when they feel included, welcomed, and treated part of the classroom community. 2. Students achieve higher academic outcomes when there are positive student-teacher relationships and a sense that an instructor cares about them."[24] Self-reflection allows educators to carefully consider student-teacher relationships, and how power imbalances can affect teaching and learning for all students (discussed in chapter 7 about Chief Joseph).

Teachers interested in using Dr. King's life and work as inspiration to promote inclusivity can benefit from taking the first step. Dr. King reminded educators: "Everybody can be great . . . because everybody can serve. You don't have to have a college degree to serve. You don't have to make your subject and your verb agree to serve. . . . You only need a heart full of grace, a soul generated by love. And you can be that servant."[25] Identification of ways to enhance classroom community and deeper knowledge of student backgrounds allows teachers to become more inclusive educators, and thus better teachers.

Dr. King was deeply strategic about his activities, demonstrations, and protests. He planned, implemented, and assessed every action with deliberation and without bias. Careful thought and preparation were habits of excellence for Dr. King, which led to personal success and organizational success for the civil rights movement. "All labor that uplifts humanity has dignity and importance and should be undertaken with painstaking excellence."[26]

INTERSECTIONS

He's doing what he's doing on the basis of conscience. He's absolutely sincere. I will strongly endorse his actions.

—Martin Luther King, Jr., on heavyweight champion boxer Muhammad Ali when he refused to join the US Army when drafted during the Vietnam War.[27]

Let the strivings of us all prove Martin Luther King Jr. to have been correct, when he said that humanity can no longer be tragically bound to the starless midnight of racism and war.

—Nelson Mandela, in his Nobel Peace Prize Acceptance Address.[28]

TEACHING SUMMARY: BE COURAGEOUS LIKE MARTIN LUTHER KING, JR.

- Recognize the interconnectedness of all individuals and groups. Providing aid to struggling students will help all students.
- Learn about people who are different from yourself by interacting with people who are different from yourself.
- Provide the right level of "tension" for maximum learning impact. Dr. King was nonviolent, but confrontational, unafraid of tension.
- Find the positive aspects of setbacks, roadblocks, and failures. View challenges as opportunities for learning that lead to fewer mistakes and greater effectiveness in the future.
- Maintain and promote optimism and hope for the future. Never give up on students or the educational process.
- Meet hatred with love.
- Recognize the relative magnitude of personal teaching trials and tribulations by reflecting on Dr. King's death threats, assaults, and murder.
- Forgive yourself for past errors and mistakes in order to serve others more effectively.
- Find deep meaning in the teaching profession and service to others to enable courage and effectiveness.

NOTES

1. King, "Integration."
2. King, "Keep Moving."
3. King, "Mountaintop."
4. King, "Mountaintop."
5. King, *Autobiography*, 7.
6. King, *Autobiography*, 7.
7. King, *Autobiography*, 12.
8. King, *Autobiography*, 14.
9. King, *Autobiography*, 26.
10. King, "Letter from Birmingham Jail," In *Autobiography*, 189.
11. King, *Stride*, 20.

12. King, *Autobiography*, 191.
13. King, "Education."
14. King, Nobel Peace Prize lecture.
15. King, *Strength*, 94.
16. King, *Stride*, 156.
17. King, *Autobiography*, 358.
18. King, *Autobiography*, 358–359.
19. King, *Autobiography*, 226.
20. King, *Strength*, 125.
21. Edelman, "Kid's First!", 77.
22. Scott, "Inclusive Educator."
23. Scott, "Inclusive Educator."
24. Scott, "Inclusive Educator."
25. King, "Drum Major."
26. King, *Strength*, 71.
27. Lapointe, "Muhammad Ali."
28. Nobel Prize website, Nelson Mandela.

REFERENCES

Edelman, Marian Wright. "Kid's First!" Martin Luther King, Jr. quoted in *Mother Jones Magazine* (May-June 1991): 77.

King, Martin Luther, Jr. *The Autobiography of Martin Luther King, Jr.* Ed. Clayborne Carson, New York: Grand Central Publishing, 2001.

King, Martin Luther, Jr. "The Drum Major Instinct," sermon at Ebenezer Baptist Church in Atlanta, Georgia, February 4, 1968.

King, Martin Luther, Jr. "The Future of Integration," address in Finney Chapel at Oberlin College, October 22, 1964, as quoted in "When MLK Came to Oberlin" by Cindy Leise, *The Chronicle-Telegram*, January 21, 2008.

King, Martin Luther, Jr. "I've Been to the Mountaintop," speech delivered at Bishop Charles Mason Temple in Memphis, Tennessee. April 3, 1968. *American Public Media*. Say it Plain: A Century of Great African American Speeches. Accessed May 17, 2021. http://americanradioworks.publicradio.org/features/sayitplain/mlk-ing.html

King, Martin Luther, Jr. "Keep Moving from this Mountain," Founders Day Address at the Sisters Chapel, Spelman College, Atlanta, Georgia, April 11, 1960. Accessed May 17, 2021. https://kinginstitute.stanford.edu/king-papers/documents/keep-moving-mountain-address-spelman-college-10-april-1960

King, Martin Luther, Jr. Nobel Peace Prize Lecture, "The Quest for Peace and Justice," Auditorium of the University of Oslo. December 11, 1964. Accessed May 18, 2021. https://www.nobelprize.org/prizes/peace/1964/king/lecture/

King, Martin Luther, Jr. "The Purpose of Education," Morehouse College, Atlanta Georgia, *Maroon Tiger* (January–February 1947): 10.

King, Martin Luther, Jr. *Strength to Love*. New York: Harper and Row, 1963.

King, Martin Luther, Jr. *Stride toward Freedom: The Montgomery Story*. New York: Harper and Brothers, 1958.

Lapointe, Joe. "Muhammad Ali Defied the Vietnam Draft 50 Years Ago Today." *Observer*, April 28, 2017. Accessed May 17, 2021. https://observer.com/2017/04 /50-years-ago-muhammad-ali-refuses-vietnam-draft/

Nobel Prize website. The Nobel Peace Prize 1993. Nelson Mandela. Accessed May 25, 2021. https://www.nobelprize.org/prizes/peace/1993/mandela/biographical/

Scott, Inara. "On Becoming a More Inclusive Educator." *The Scholarly Teacher*, September 10, 2020. Accessed May 20, 2021. https://www.scholarlyteacher.com/ post/on-becoming-a-more-inclusive-educator

Chapter 12

Triumph from Pain

Frida Kahlo

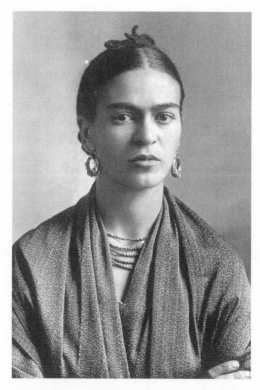

Figure 12.1 **Frida Kahlo.** *Source*: Wikimedia Commons. Guillermo Kahlo.

My painting carries with it the message of pain.

—Frida Kahlo[1]

I think that little by little I'll be able to solve my problems and survive.

—Frida Kahlo [2]

At the end of the day, we can endure much more than we think we can.

—Frida Kahlo [3]

CHAPTER SYNOPSIS

Frida Kahlo faced enormous physical, emotional, and relational challenges throughout her life and career as an artist. Her inspiring life story provides effective motivation for educators to use their own unique talents and personalities to minimize the effects of life struggles and promote student understanding and achievement. Kahlo's insistence on staying true to herself yielded both amazing art and a large positive impact on the world. Teachers have much to learn from Frida's joy, strength, and intensity.

Frida Kahlo (1907–1954) was an iconic Mexican artist, highly regarded for her ability to capture physical pain, emotional turmoil, and marital anguish in her artwork. Her art and life story are increasingly popular and her image is well-known. She is celebrated throughout the world by her first name: Frida. Her paintings include fifty-five self-portraits treasured by art historians, admired by museum visitors, and widely recognized in popular culture. Her ground-breaking art blends Mexican traditions, folk art, and religious images.

Viewers often find it difficult to divert their eyes from Frida's paintings: vibrant colors capture an astonishing intensity. The paintings portray pain, anguish, joy, and love in a unique and striking way, easily distinguishable from other artists' work. Frida's art has led to a huge amount of international attention and notoriety: "Fridamania."

Frida's iconic image is emblazoned on shirts, posters, coffee mugs, and countless trinkets sold to tourists, art fans, and multitudes inspired by Frida's life, art, and meaning. Biographer Elizabeth Bakewell concluded: "During her lifetime Frida Kahlo, the person and the personage, was a symbol of human suffering and emotional strength."[4]

Frida's father was a German Jewish photographer of Hungarian descent, and her mother was Mexican of both European and indigenous descent. Her diverse ethnic background provided a major theme of her paintings, where she explored the complexities of Mexico's multiethnic heritage, colonialism, and revolution. Elizabeth Bakewell states, "Frida Kahlo mixed Indian with

European, art with craft, high with low, crossing from one strata to the other with little regard for such elite constructions of difference. . . . Rather than mask her racial and cultural hybridism, as other members of the elite did, Kahlo openly acknowledged hers."[5]

PAIN

Frida enjoyed a happy but brief childhood, followed by a life of pain, suffering, over thirty surgeries, relationship issues, and persistent turmoil. At age six, Frida contracted polio that deformed her right leg. Rather than succumb to her unfortunate circumstances, Frida did not change her activities, attitude, or life. In spite of her polio-stricken leg, she became a strong athlete before the age of ten, good at running, wrestling, boxing, and other sports.[6] Frida studied biology and anatomy in the hopes of becoming a medical doctor. Her deep knowledge of the human body and medicine later became a major theme of her artwork.

Frida said, "Nothing is absolute. Everything changes, everything moves, everything revolves, everything flies and goes away."[7] At age eighteen, a severe accident forced a drastic change on Frida's life. While riding home from school, Frida's bus was hit by a trolley car. The accident broke Frida's back in three places, pulverized her collarbone and pelvis, broke her right leg, and resulted in numerous fractures in both feet. She was impaled by a metal rod through her abdomen and vagina. Frida suffered from immense pain for the rest of her life, with frequent and debilitating medical procedures, including amputation of her right leg.

Frida defied her pain, using it as the foundation for becoming a major artist and adored celebrity icon: "What doesn't kill me, nourishes me."[8] Mother Teresa battled intense emotional pain but overcame it by actively pursuing her ideals of helping others (chapter 4). Educators facing personal or occupational pain can benefit from the example set by Teresa and Frida to use the pain to improve the world for others.

Frida was bedridden for over a year. She shifted her activity from sports to painting, and her career goal from medicine to art. While in bed, Frida became accomplished at painting. She painted herself and her pain, resulting in what is considered by many to be among the best paintings ever created. Frida's art now appears in the most prominent art museums of the world. Frida broke boundaries as a female artist and as a Mexican artist. Rather than rejecting Mexican folk art, traditions, and culture, Frida celebrated her ethnic heritage in her clothing, hairstyle, jewelry, painting, and lifestyle.

At the time of Frida's life, Diego Rivera was the most prominent artist in Mexico. Frida met Diego when he was painting a mural at her high school.

They fell deeply in love, and Frida married Diego in 1929. Frida was twenty years of age, Diego was forty-two. Frida remained married to Diego until her death in 1954; the relationship involved significant heartbreak, multiple extramarital affairs, separations, divorce, and remarriage. Their relationship was passionate, but difficult. They remained together because each respected and admired the other's art, intelligence, and personality.

Diego, well known for romance, took many lovers during his marriage to Frida. Although she was deeply hurt by Diego's behavior, Frida did her best to overlook it. This changed when Diego had an affair with Frida's younger sister Cristina. This unfaithfulness destroyed Diego's relationship with Frida, resulting in divorce then remarriage one year later. Diego was a central figure in Frida's paintings as both an admired lover and source of pain. Frida had several miscarriages that resulted from her injuries from the accident and remained childless.

Frida's art captured not only the emotional pain from her chaotic marriage but also the physical pain from polio and the trolley accident. The intense quality of Frida's paintings became recognized and admired. The Surrealists, a group of French artists who painted eccentric dreamscapes, wanted to include her work as part of their movement. Frida would not be labeled: "They thought I was a Surrealist, but I wasn't. I never painted dreams. I painted my own reality."[9] Frida explained the motivation for using herself as a model: "I paint myself because I am alone. I am the subject I know best."[10]

The great Mexican writer Carlos Fuentes concluded that "Frida Kahlo, as no other artist of our tortured century, translated pain into art. She suffered thirty-two operations from the day of her accident to the day of her death. Her biography consists of twenty-nine years of pain."[11] Diego Rivera glorified Frida, declaring: "endurance of truth, reality, cruelty, and suffering. Never before had a woman put such agonized poetry on canvas."[12] And yet, somehow, Frida was a joyful person.

ALEGRIA

The English translation for the Spanish word *Alegria* is "joy," or "cheerfulness." Frida was well known for her outsized joy, humor, and laughter throughout her life. Like Anne Frank, Frida recorded her private thoughts, ideas, and desires in a diary (chapter 10). Carlos Fuentes wrote that Frida's diary recorded "her joy, her fun, her fantastic imagination."[13] Fuentes reported that as a child, Frida was teased, taunted, and ridiculed for her deformity. Neither the physical limitations of her shrunken right leg nor her mean-spirited classmates defeated Frida. What a powerful role model for teachers!

Albert Camus observed absurdity in the human condition, but rejected it in favor of happiness (chapter 6). Like Frida, Mahatma Gandhi believed that all actions should be undertaken with great joy (chapter 9): "Joy lies in the fight, in the attempt, in the suffering involved, not in the victory itself."[14] The transformation of pain into joy is a major theme of many successful people throughout the ages, and thus provides strong motivation for educators. Frida pronounced, "There is nothing more precious than laughter."[15]

Psychologists have found that joy is a social, rather than an individual experience. Organizational psychologist Adam Grant states: "emotions are inherently social: They're woven through our interactions. Research has found that people laugh five times as often when they're with others as when they're alone. . . . Peak happiness lies mostly in collective activity."[16]

Pioneering sociologist Emile Durkheim called this, "collective effervescence." This idea can be used to explain the social nature of Frida's belief: "It is strength to laugh and to abandon oneself, to be light."[17] Durkheim claimed that we find our greatest happiness in social settings, from the energy and harmony people feel during a shared experience.

Adam Grant explains: "Psychologists find that in cultures where people pursue happiness individually, they may actually become lonelier. But in cultures where they pursue happiness socially—through connecting, caring, and contributing—people appear to be more likely to gain well-being."[18] Frida believed that: "Tragedy is the most ridiculous thing."[19]

TEACHING

Frida taught art throughout her career. One of Frida's first students, Fanny Rabel (Fanny Rabinovich at the time), explained that Frida was "instinctive, spontaneous. She would become happy in front of any beautiful thing."[20] Frida's enjoyment of both her subject matter and life itself made a large, lasting, positive difference for her students.

Student Arturo Garcia Bustos remembered one occasion when Frida: "We were all in love with Frida. She had a special grace and attraction. She was so *alegre* [joyful] that she made poetry around her."[21] Frida's joy was memorable, meaningful, and a central feature of Frida's personality and energy. Teachers who make an effort to share joy with others will be rewarded with fun, positivity, and improved student learning outcomes. Joy and cheerfulness provide a solid emotional foundation that allows students to focus their energy on learning. The desire to learn is greatly enhanced when the subject matter is interpreted in a fun and cheerful fashion.

In 1943, Frida began a teaching job at "La Esmerelda," the Ministry of Public Education's School of Painting and Sculpture, where she taught for a decade. Fanny Rabel recalls being skeptical of Frida, as she had been told that Frida did not know how to teach: "But the moment that I met Frida I was fascinated because she had a gift to fascinate people. She was unique. She had enormous *alegria* [joy], humor and love of life."[22]

Frida utilized the challenge and support theory of student development. She explained to her students on the first day of class: "it is certain that to paint is the most terrific thing that there is, but to do it well is very difficult, it is necessary to do it, to learn the skill very well, to have very strict self-discipline and above all to have love, to feel a great love for painting."[23]

Frida's challenge to her students reflects Dr. Martin Luther King's emphasis on finding a life purpose, which provides strength and courage during times of adversity (chapter 11). When educators identify the underlying motivation and purpose for their work, it enables them to teach courageously with the conviction that, as Frida and Dr. King, they are doing the right thing.

Frida was enthusiastic, as reported by her students: "She'd say, 'How well you painted this!' or 'This part came out very ugly.' What she taught us, fundamentally, was love of the people, and a taste for popular art."[24] Frida radiated enthusiasm as suggested by Nelson Mandela (chapter 8). By being positive and enthusiastic, even when in pain, Frida overcame the suffering and made relentless joy a feature of her personality and teaching.

Frida began her teaching assignment with a large class, but due to increasingly difficult health problems, became unable to commute from her home to the school. Biographer Raquel Tibol clarified, "The tyrannical demands of a torn body made her return to confinement from which she had tried to escape. But being with the young people brought her a joy she did not want to give up, so she kept on teaching and managed to have the classes continue in her home."[25] The students commuted to Frida's house, and a group of three boys and one girl continued the course, "all fanatically enthusiastic about the teaching methods of that unique teacher."[26]

Frida's group of young admirers came to be called, "Los Fridos." After Frida's death, Rivera wrote: "Frida shaped students who today figure among the most valued men and women artists of Mexico. She always encouraged them to preserve and develop their personalities in their work and in the social and political clarification of their ideas."[27] The group worked together with Frida on projects, including murals and joint exhibitions.

Frida encouraged, supported, and promoted Los Fridos in every way possible, and the artists became successful professionals under her enthusiastic instruction and coaching. Los Fridos began as a group of four students but grew to an organization of forty-seven painters called the Young

Revolutionary Artists. Frida had a huge positive impact on her students. Fanny Rabel concludes that, "Frida's great teaching was to see through artist's eyes, to open our eyes to the world, to see Mexico, she did not influence us through her way of painting, but through her way of living, of looking at the world and at people and at art."[28]

Chief Joseph modeled positivity while fighting for the survival of the Nez Perce people. Joseph shared his positive energy with both natives and whites throughout his life (chapter 7). Frida left an amazing legacy for teachers who desire to help students! Educators who model enthusiasm for the subject matter and joy in life can have a huge impact within the classroom and beyond school. Frida's student emphasizes an important characteristic of good teaching: Frida's iconic personality and approach to life mattered more than the subject matter.

ICON

Frida spent many months in a body cast in bed, and a great deal of time in a wheelchair. Yet she was able to capture the attention of nearly everyone she met and interacted with, and after her death, the admiration of the world. Historian Liza Bakewell informed readers that "Kahlo's reaction to her own handicaps and the teasing she received from her cohorts was to foster her strong personality."[29]

Kahlo invented and promoted her own identity in art, style, fashion, and expression based on indigenous Mexican traditions, folk art style, and Mexican history. Years later, Bob Dylan used folk art rather than sophistication to create his own persona (chapter 2). Diego purchased a Tehauna outfit for Frida in southern Mexico. These outfits, non-tailored and brightly colored, became Frida's hallmark. The shirts are embroidered, and the skirts are long and flowing. Frida wore Tehauna outfits in public and painted herself wearing them. Bakewell suggested that the outfits, "suited her physical needs, her political agenda, and her strong personality."[30]

The loose clothing covered her polio-stricken leg, her broken back, and her painful feet. Tehauna dresses symbolized her strong ideology of Mexican nationalism and traditions. Tehauna women were the leaders of a matriarchal society, and the dresses represent female leadership and confidence. Liza Bakewell explains, "Submerging her body in Tehauna fabrics, Kahlo gave to herself an aura of empowerment and other-worldliness, especially when she traveled to New York and to Paris; they were neither of her class nor of her time."[31]

Frida's art, fashion, and personality were all based on Mexican roots, rather than European themes; female empowerment; and folk painting instead of elite artistic methods. These traits resulted in a unique, unforgettable persona: Frida became iconic in her work and in her life. In 1938, Frida had her first one-woman show in New York, and was featured on the cover of *Vogue* magazine. One year later, she had a one-woman show in Paris.

Educators can benefit from being iconic. Students who recognize teacher traits, sayings, and images will often appreciate the uniqueness of a teacher's "brand." In some cases, teachers have bold and assertive reputations, like Frida. Muhammad Ali used his enormous speaking ability, physical power, grace, beauty, and sharp commentary to form an unforgettable persona that people would love or love to hate (chapter 1). Conversely, Fred Rogers used kindness, a gentle manner, a sweater, and tennis shoes to create a recognizable, notable identity (chapter 3). Teachers can use almost any repeated phrase, attire, or action to become "iconic."

As her fame increased, "Kahlo became an extrovert, building friendships in the most public of circles, while simultaneously becoming an introvert, retreating into herself through her writing and her painting."[32] Like many icons, her public image and actions differed from her private life and work. Teachers do not have to sacrifice their private identity to publicly share iconic joy and positivity with students.

Author Carlos Fuentes described how Frida "upstaged everything and everybody" at the opera by entering The Palace of Fine Arts in Mexico City as an Aztec Goddess: "The laces, the ribbons, the skirts, the rustling petticoats, the braids, the moonlike headdresses opening up her face like the wings of a dark butterfly: Frida Kahlo, showing us all that suffering could not wither, nor sickness stale, her infinite variety."[33]

CONCLUSION

Teachers are constrained in many ways: physical pain, emotional turmoil, personal challenges, and relationship difficulties. Frida provides nourishment for the weary and inspiration for the disillusioned. Frida not only survived her physical, emotional, and personal pain, but she flourished because of it. Frida used her unusual personal and physical circumstances to live well, be a successful artist, and become an iconic leader and trend setter.

In the same way, teachers can use their constraints, pain, and struggles as springboards to greatness. Frida's iconic images, clothing, style, irrepressible positive energy, humor, and paintings show the way to teach and live. In 1953, Diego Rivera revealed, "It isn't tragedy that governs Frida's work . . . the darkness of her pain is merely a velvety background for the marvelous light of her biological strength, her superfine sensitivity, shining intelligence, and invincible strength to struggle for just being alive."[34]

The talented film director Orson Welles proposed that, "The enemy of art is the absence of limitations."[35] Welles believed that creativity and success were sparked by a fight against difficulties. Malcolm X became angry when he experienced injustice in his personal life and in society as a whole. He used the anger to become convicted to improve the world (chapter 5). Malcolm's anger catalyzed his leadership that left a significant impact on the world.

Fred Rogers taught children that, "The greatest gift you ever give is your honest self."[36] In Frida's case, this was art: "I am not sick. I am broken. But I am happy to be alive as long as I can paint."[37] Frida, like Sisyphus, found joy in her burden of pain, and shared with friends, students, and family. Teachers who desire to improve the lives of others can share iconic joy with their students: joy for learning, joy for the subject matter, joy for each other, and joy for life.

INTERSECTIONS

There is no normal life that is free of pain. It's the very wrestling with our problems that can be the impetus for our growth.

—Fred Rogers[38]

The entire performance felt like . . . a reiteration of the deep, overwhelming, and practical utility of art to combat pain.

—Petrusich on Patti Smith's Nobel Prize ceremony honoring Bob Dylan.[39]

A sick child is much more than his or her sickness.

—Fred Rogers[40]

TEACHING SUMMARY. TRIUMPH OVER PAIN LIKE FRIDA KAHLO

- Model how to transform human suffering into emotional strength. Frida transformed the darkness of personal pain into triumph: "What doesn't kill me, nourishes me."
- Celebrate cultural hybridism by demonstrating how learning and life are improved with a diversity of backgrounds, interests, and opinions.
- Authenticity. Teach what you know well. Teach your own reality, and the subject that you know best.

- Icon. Be an iconic teacher by creating your own "brand." Personalized clothing, sayings, or habits are good ways to distinguish you and your teaching.
- *Alegria.* Teach with great joy, enthusiasm, and cheerfulness. This will make the largest positive in the world!

NOTES

1. Ahuja, *Pocket*, 6.
2. Ahuja, *Pocket*, 19.
3. Ahuja, *Pocket*, 66.
4. Bakewell, "Frida Kahlo," 315.
5. Bakewell, "Frida Kahlo," 317.
6. Bakewell, "Frida Kahlo," 316.
7. Ahuja, *Pocket*, 64.
8. Ahuja, *Pocket*, 21.
9. Ahuja, *Pocket*, 10.
10. Herrera, *Frida*, 14.
11. Fuentes, "Introduction," 12.
12. Fuentes, "Introduction," 13.
13. Fuentes, "Introduction," 10.
14. Gandhi, *Day Book.*
15. Ahuja, *Pocket*, 65.
16. Grant, *Kind of Joy.*
17. Ahuja, *Pocket*, 73.
18. Grant, *Kind of Joy.*
19. Ahuja, *Pocket*, 68.
20. Herrera, *Frida*, 332.
21. Herrera, *Frida*, 333.
22. Herrera, *Frida*, 329.
23. Herrera, *Frida*, 330.
24. Herrera, *Frida*, 331.
25. Tibol, *Open Life*, 180.
26. Tibol, *Open Life*, 181.
27. Tibol, *Open Life*, 181.
28. Herrera, *Frida*, 331.
29. Bakewell, "Frida Kahlo," 315.
30. Bakewell, "Frida Kahlo," 316.
31. Bakewell, "Frida Kahlo," 316.
32. Bakewell, "Frida Kahlo," 315.
33. Fuentes, "Introduction," 8.
34. Tibol, *Open Life*, 7.
35. Jaglom, *Independent Filmmaker*, 78.

36. Rogers, *Wisdom*, 43.
37. Ahuja, *Pocket*, 13.
38. Rogers, "Quotes."
39. Petrusich, "Patti Smith."
40. Rogers, *Life's Journeys.*

REFERENCES

Ahuja, Molly, Ed. *Pocket Frida Kahlo Wisdom.* London: Hardie Grant Books, 2018.

Bakewell, Elizabeth. "Frida Kahlo." In *Concise Encyclopedia of Mexico*, ed. Michael Werner. Chicago: Fitzroy Dearborn Publishers, 2001.

Fuentes, "Introduction." In *The Diary of Frida Kahlo: An Intimate Self-Portrait*, ed. Frida Kahlo, New York: Abrams, 1995, 7–24.

Gandhi, Mahatma. *A Day Book of Thoughts from Mahatma Gandhi*, ed. Char K. T. Narasimha. Kolkata, India: Macmillan & Co., 1951.

Grant, Adam. "There's a Specific Kind of Joy We've Been Missing." *New York Times*, July 10, 2021. Accessed July 14, 2021. https://www.nytimes.com/2021/07/10/opinion/sunday/covid-group-emotions-happiness.html

Herrera, Hayden. *Frida: A Biography of Frida Kahlo.* New York: Harper Perennial, 1983.

Jaglom, Henry. "The Independent Filmmaker." In *The Movie Business Book*, ed. Jason E. Squire, Second Edition, 78. New York: Fireside: Simon & Schuster, 1992.

Petrusich, Amanda. "A Transcendent Patti Smith Accepts Bob Dylan's Nobel Prize." *The New Yorker*, December 10, 2016. https://www.newyorker.com/culture/cultural-comment/a-transcendent-patti-smith-accepts-bob-dylans-nobel-prize

Rogers, Fred. *Life's Journeys According to Mister Rogers: Things to Remember Along the Way.* New York: Hachette Books; Revised edition, 2019, 33.

Rogers, Fred. "Mr. Rogers Quotes: Wisdom from the Children's Television Host on His Birthday." *Newsweek*, Nina Godlewski, March 20 2018. Accessed July 3, 2021. https://www.newsweek.com/fred-rogers-birthday-quotes-wont-you-be-my-neighbor-movie-854013

Rogers, Fred. *Wisdom from the World According to Mister Rogers: Important Things to Remember.* White Plains, NY: Peter Pauper Press, 2006.

Tibol, Raquel. *Frida Kahlo: An Open Life.* Translated by Elinor Randal. Albuquerque, NM: University of New Mexico Press, 1983.

Acknowledgments

Thanks to my current and former students at K-State. What a pleasure and honor to work with such great people!

Thank you to the highly professional and supportive editors at Rowman and Littlefield: Tom Koerner, Carlie Wall, and Mark Kerr.

I am so appreciative of my teacher friends who contributed to the review process. The book was greatly improved by feedback, suggestions, and ideas from: Peter Chadwick, John Crespi, Penelope Diebel, Greg Eiselein, Chris Herald, Angela Hubler, Justin Kastner, Marla Lohmann, Kris Nelson, Cindy Norris, Larry Rodgers, Susan Jackson Rodgers, Caela Simmons-Wood, Dawn Weigel Stiegert, and Na Zuo.

It is a great joy to share teaching ideas and experiences with other teachers! Writing this book resulted in numerous fun and productive conversations about teaching, learning, and writing with many intelligent, caring, and professional friends and colleagues! Thank you! Keep going!

Huge gratitude to my family: Mary Ellen, Katie, Charles, and Deneige Barkley. Thank you for your enduring patience, reinforcement, and love.

Index

About the Author

Andrew Barkley is professor and University Distinguished Teaching Scholar in the Department of Agricultural Economics at Kansas State University. He has enjoyed teaching at Kansas State University, the University of Cambridge in Cambridge, England, the University of Arizona, Quaid-I-Azam University in Islamabad, Pakistan, and the University of Chicago.